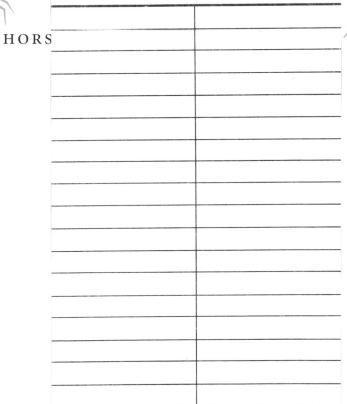

HORS

DATE DUE

BRODART

Cat. No. 23-221

HORSE OPERA

*The Strange History of
the 1930s Singing Cowboy*

Peter Stanfield

UNIVERSITY OF ILLINOIS PRESS

URBANA AND CHICAGO

© 2002 by the Board of Trustees
of the University of Illinois
All rights reserved
Manufactured in the United States of America
1 2 3 4 5 C P 5 4 3 2 1

Library of Congress Cataloging-in-Publication Data
Stanfield, Peter, 1958–
Horse opera : the strange history of the 1930s singing cowboy /
Peter Stanfield.
    p.   cm.
Includes bibliographical references and index.
ISBN 0-252-02733-7 (cloth : alk. paper)
ISBN 0-252-07049-6 (paper : alk. paper)
1. Western films—United States—History and criticism.
2. Motion picture actors and actresses—United States—Biography.
3. Country musicians—United States—Biography.
I. Title.
PN1995.9.W4S83   2002
791.43'6278—dc21   2001005008

DEDICATED TO FRANCES AND AGNES RAE,

TWO STARS IN MY BLUE HEAVEN

I'm going to town, honey, what you want me to bring you back?
I want a pint of booze and a John B. Stetson hat.

   —Jimmie Rodgers, "Blue Yodel #8"

CONTENTS

PREFACE

This work first began to take shape in an essay that I wrote for Ed Buscombe and Roberta Pearson's collection *Back in the Saddle Again: New Essays on the Western* (1998) and then developed for my book *Hollywood, Westerns, and the 1930s: The Lost Trail* (2001). The latter contextualized the series western within a history of Hollywood's cycles and trends that focused on A-feature western productions. It became apparent in researching and writing the chapters on series westerns that the figure of the singing cowboy warranted a specific study in order to chart fully the complexity of his cultural and production history. *Horse Opera,* then, provides a more extensive arena in which to do this. Using the industrial context of Hollywood production already established in previous work, this volume substantially expands its critical examination of the 1930s singing cowboy to address those dimensions that are historically specific to him: literary and performance antecedents, legacies from silent cinema, the development of commercial music media, and the prevailing conditions of film production that made the series western.

A huge debt of gratitude must go to Ed Buscombe, who has been with the project from start to finish and from whom I received exceptional support and guidance while writing this book.

I must also acknowledge the help that Richard Maltby has given to this and other ventures of mine during the past several years. Peter Kramer also gave generously of his time and thoughts.

I carried out primary research principally at the British Film Institute library in London and at the Autry Museum of Western Heritage, Los Angeles, and was funded by grants from the United Kingdom's Southampton Institute of Higher Education. For giving me access to rare material and for being gracious hosts during my research trip to Los Angeles, I remain particularly indebted to Alex Gordon and Karla Buhlman at Gene Autry Entertainment, which licenses the use of Autry's image, music, and films.

My greatest debt is to Esther Sonnet, my co-conspirator and collaborator. She read and rewrote this book countless times. Esther, without you, this would be nothing.

In addition to the motley crew mentioned throughout, I wrote this book to a soundtrack provided by Pussy Galore, the modern reverberations of Don Howland's Bassholes, and the StripKings (London).

Nos haec novimus esse nihil.

HORSE OPERA

INTRODUCTION

Keep them Clean

While I was researching and writing this book, the two most celebrated singing cowboys died. Roy Rogers passed away on July 6, 1998, and Gene Autry followed three months later on October 2. Their deaths were succeeded by those of two smaller stars of the singing western: Eddie Dean on March 4, 1999, and Rex Allen on December 17, 1999. Of the others, Tex Ritter died in 1974, Dick Foran in 1979, Smith Ballew in 1984, Jimmy Wakely in 1982, Fred Scott in 1991, Ray Whitley in 1979, and Tex Fletcher (who starred in only one film) in 1987. As I was editing the finished manuscript, Dale Evans, the "queen" to Roy Rogers's "king," died on February 7, 2001. As of this writing, only Monte Hale and Herb Jeffries, a one-time featured vocalist with Duke Ellington's Orchestra and star of four sepia westerns, survive. All of them, though, outlived the phenomenon of the singing western, which lasted little more than two decades, from 1934 to 1956.

This is not a book about endings but, rather, I hope, of beginnings. Despite the relatively short life span of the singing western, this book concerns only the films produced during the 1930s and with their cultural antecedents in literature, silent film, and popular music. The horse opera of the 1930s, I argue, had a unique relationship with its core audience: rural or newly urban working-class families that experienced the hardship of the Great Depression and felt the economic pressures to adapt to new ways of living. My primary aim is to understand an aspect of western film production that scholarly histories of the genre have roundly ignored. This is also a study of a low cultural form that was marketed to an economically disenfranchised audience, and to this end I draw upon recent work in U.S. cultural studies that is concerned with examining issues of class and race as manifested within mass forms of popular entertainment. An analysis of the singing western that fails to recognize and draw out the rich and complex cultural history upon which that genre is based would inevitably repeat clichés and stereotypes.

Though cowboys had sung in the movies after Hollywood convert-ed to synchronized sound in the late 1920s, the figure of the singing cowboy as a distinct film persona did not emerge until the radio star Gene Autry appeared in starring roles in the Mascot serial *The Phan-tom Empire* (1935) and the feature film *Tumbling Tumbleweeds* (Repub-lic, 1935). More than anyone else, Autry defined the singing cowboy, and by the end of the 1930s he was one of Hollywood's biggest box-office draws. The obituaries of Rogers and Autry attempted to explain the attraction of these "essentially ludicrous" figures to an audience that had not grown up watching singing westerns. One writer described the singing cowboy's mind-set this way: "Them bandits have beaten my mother, ravished my girl, burned down my house, killed my cattle and blinded my best friend. I'm goin' to get 'em if it's the last thing I do. But first, folks, I'm going to sing you a little song."[1] The singing cow-boy's muse, it appeared, transcended all worldly concerns, including lustful temptation. Autry, it was said, "was never seen to kiss his lead-ing lady unless she was a horse."[2] This aside, Autry helped fix the sing-ing cowboy as a persona free of moral turpitude when he published his "Cowboy Code," ten commandments enjoining truthfulness, kind-ness, tolerance, cleanliness in thought and deed, respect for others, and patriotism. By 1939 Autry was pledging to his audience that he would never make a "picture that you won't be proud to take your son, daughter, mother or father to see. I'll keep them clean."[3] The absurd narratives, the preponderance of musical moments, and the exposi-tion of a morally sanitized universe that could appeal only to "very young children and middle-aged women" have conspired to ensure that the singing cowboy has received only the scantiest of scholarly or popular attention.[4] The view of the singing cowboy as little more than a Saturday matinee distraction for kids, a nostalgic figure for more innocent times, or, more recently, a prime example of American camp has effaced his real history.

This book aims to challenge such preconceptions—to question the critical shibboleths that have built up around the singing cowboy and the series western. My objective is to retrieve the contemporary context for these films, to view them not in isolation but within the cultural and performance traditions from which they developed, to attempt to understand who was the audience for them and how the films addressed that audience. I make a claim for the singing cowboy as more than just a cultural curio or marginalia in histories of western representations. I argue that he is one of the most important cultural figures to emerge from the tumultuous years of the Great Depression—a character that represented the fantasies, desires, and ambitions of those who felt keenly the economic hardship and the threat (and fact) of dispossession and dislocation. Through an examination of the singing cowboy's antecedents in literature and silent film, of the media industries in which he was produced, of his intended contemporary audience, of the performance traditions within which he worked, and the performance traditions of the films of the 1930s, this study reclaims the contexts within which the singing cowboy was produced and consumed.

The singing cowboy, far from being of interest largely to children, made a powerful appeal to segments of the film audience that mainstream Hollywood did not address, or did not address directly. In particular, his films dramatized social and political questions and did so largely from the point of view of those whom the depression had deprived. These movies used artistic strategies that did not accord with established aesthetic principles of middle-class good taste. In doing so, the singing cowboy apparently broke with the tradition of the western that Hollywood had inherited from literary culture. But this makes a number of assumptions about who and what the cowboy was, where he came from, and what he meant. I argue that it is possible to trace a different line of development, one that sees the cowboy as open for a more radical interpretation, and one that leads more directly to the singing cowboy than does the received notion of the cowboy's origin. This is why I begin by examining the genealogy of the cowboy in turn-of-the-century fiction. Rather than uphold the common view, that Owen Wister's *The Virginian* (1902) first and most successfully essayed the archetype of the twentieth-century western, I consider this novel to have represented an embourgeoisement of the western—a middle-class appropriation of the cowboy, who had previously entertained the masses in such déclassé forms as the dime novel. The series western reclaimed the cowboy for the mob—that inchoate mass of working-class men and women that members of America's elite, such as Wister, so vocally damned and feared. Not *The Virginian* but dime novels, magazine fiction aimed at a newly emerging professional middle class, and, significantly, novels that offered a peculiarly female address in their representation of the cowboy, provided the antecedent of the singing cowboy.

The turn-of-the-century cowboy was not a homogeneous figure—he wore a number of costumes that were cut to suit the distinct demands of a heterogeneous readership divided by class, race, and gender. I trace these contending claims of ownership by reviewing cultural histories of the western that highlight the issue of class. I expand upon this analysis by considering how race and gender further aid in the production of a diverse readership for westerns. Chapter 1 concludes with an examination of the cowboy as a site of visual pleasure. Although the various narratives have distinctive perspectives on class, race, and gender, all share a fascination with the cowboy as a site of spectacle, an idea that takes on particular importance with his representation in film.

I begin chapter 2 by examining the cowboy as he appeared in the single-reel films of the 1900s and 1910s and then focus more sharply on how he appealed to a working-class audience. From this perspective, we can best understand the cowboy as a character type able to mediate conflicts between capital and labor, modernity and tradition, industry and agriculture, urban and rural lifestyles. Contrary to popular belief, during the 1920s the cowboy did not appeal predominantly to an adolescent male sensibility. Evidence drawn from press books and trade reviews of the films suggests that producers concentrated their marketing strategies on family audiences, stressing attractions that would draw both adult male and female patrons.

The idea that the studios designed these films for children is a misconception based on middle-class notions of what constitutes an engaging and entertaining narrative. Rather, they aimed the series western at working-class audiences, which placed comparatively little value on the logic of the narrative and the psychology of the characters. The audience for the series western primarily valued performance: stunt and trick riding, fistfights, slapstick comedy, rituals of courtship, and a complex play with character identity that promises easy movement across social and cultural boundaries—in contradistinction to the relatively fixed class and gender positions that mainstream Hollywood productions expounded.

The high valuation given to the play with character identity and performance is particularly marked in the series western's use of music. Chapter 3 examines the emergence of cowboy singers and their songs. As an adjunct of American folk music, cowboy songs were inextricably tied to a rapidly developing commercial music industry. The genre was not widely recognized by a broad U.S. public until the mid- to late 1920s, when the emerging recording industry (and other interested parties) sought to use it as a counter, or alternative, to jazz. The development and exploitation of a distinct rural market for radio gave even greater emphasis to singers able to effectively masquerade as cowboys. Besides countering the disruptive modern effects of jazz, the cowboy singers offered a more benign, respectable, *and* modern rural identity than did more vulgar vernacular music styles. Relying on sponsorship deals, radio found the figure of the cowboy to be eminently suitable for the endorsement of products targeted at rural and small town markets. The singing cowboys of the airwaves, in particular, proved to have an enduring appeal to female consumers—radio's prime target.

By the mid-1930s the singing cowboy had become the most significant figure used by radio to attract audiences and consumers from the rural regions. Furthermore, the singing cowboy acted as a synergistic agent that linked various arms of the media industries: recording, radio, publishing, live performance, and film. The key players in this field were Herbert J. Yates and Gene Autry. Yates controlled the largest of the independent film studios, Republic Pictures, and had considerable holdings in the phonograph industry. Through the agency of Yates's various commercial interests, Autry, who had begun his professional career as a singer of mountain and blues songs in the style of Jimmie Rodgers, would achieve a media profile unmatched by any contemporary cowboy singers and performers of a rural American vernacular.

Chapter 4 examines the industrial context for the production of series westerns and the eventual exploitation of cowboy singers, a field that Autry helped to define and dominate. Series westerns (or what would later become more commonly known as B westerns) were conceived and organized around a particular cowboy star and produced for independent theaters and chains whose principal market was in rural, small-town, and urban neighborhoods. Only at the close of the 1930s would some of Gene Autry's films play at first-run metropolitan houses, but this did not mean that his films (and other westerns produced by either the big or independent studios) would inevitably play on the lower half of the bill, giving them a "B" status. Gene Autry's films for Republic were headline features that enabled his company to practice the same block-booking policy as the major studios. If a theater chain wanted Gene Autry's latest season of films, it would have to book the rest of Republic's output, sight unseen. Though it is now common currency to call Autry's films B westerns, only on runs subsequent to their initial release would they play at the bottom of a bill. Contemporary terminology labeled these films as simply westerns. Prestige productions by the major studios that used top-rank stars were not called westerns but instead were marketed by a number of relatively vague generic descriptors: "action-adventure," "romance," "outdoor dramas," and the like. This hybridity registered the producers' desire to be generically inclusive of their audience's preferences. The series westerns, in contrast, had a predetermined audience that the film companies recognized in their more direct, limited, and unambiguous marketing campaigns.

Gene Autry's first film appearance was in a musical sequence in a Ken Maynard feature for the low-budget Poverty Row studio Mascot Pictures. Audiences already knew his name from his radio appearances, and Autry quickly made the shift from cameo to star. His rapid rise to success derived from his ability through song and performance to credibly suggest that he was part of the community that constituted his core audience. I examine this act of integration in chapter 5, where I pay particular attention to the role and importance of musical performance in the films. The star and his sidekick evoked and developed historical performance traditions, notably blackface minstrelsy, to connect with their audience.

In chapter 6, I continue the theme of performance tradition and focus on the use of disguise and hidden identity that structured so many of the series westerns' narratives. My concern is with understanding what the function and appeal of this endlessly repeated trope was for the western's audience. To this end I evoke some of the theories that scholars use to explain the dissembling of identity in dime novels as well as those used to explain the play with masks in blackface minstrelsy. I argue that in this context the films rehearsed the story of the American republic—a tale that gave to its participants a sense of importance in a world that worked so tirelessly to deny individual expression and agency. The mask of the cowboy was in fact an elaborate masquerade for articulating the fears and desires of the working-class audience. Similarly, western settings and situations act as a mask for contemporary environments and concerns. This is why so many series westerns have a modern setting, or, at least, are situated in a world that is *not* readily identifiable as either the historical or modern West. Autry's films, in particular, deal overtly with issues engendered by the Great Depression and the New Deal. They make no claim to represent the West authentically, but they do invoke the economic, social, and cultural issues that most affected his core constituency.

The lack of critical attention given to series westerns has meant that critics have entirely overlooked the role of women, as featured in the films, in the films' production, and in the consumption of the films. The figure of the young heroine is most overtly responsible for representing modernity. Independent, wage earning, and almost inevitably dressed in contemporary fashions, she confronts not only received critical wisdom about the representation of women in the western but also the notion that the series western is ideologically reactionary. The series western is not a retrogressive reaction to modernity and its discontents but a confrontation that attempts to mediate between a world that seems to be both ever changing and stagnantly traditional.

In 1939 all the major studios made a commitment to the production of prestige westerns that would not waver until the late 1950s. For the first time since the 1920s the film industry used the western to cater not only to rural and small-town patrons but also to first-run metropolitan audiences. Moreover, by 1940 Autry's appeal for audiences had broadened and deepened to such an extent that he had become the first cowboy star to cross over and appear in *Motion Picture Herald*'s poll of the top-ten box-office attractions—arriving, as if from nowhere, at number four. The event stunned the fan magazine press, which, until the big studios employed their top male matinee stars in westerns in 1939, had all but ignored the genre and given only cursory coverage to Autry. The press ran wild with the story of Autry's elevation to the top flight of stars, valiantly attempting to explain his appeal. Autry and the western had moved from the margins of U.S. culture to the center—an event that had been played out six months earlier when Autry, on a personal appearance tour of the British Isles and Ireland, rode his horse Champion into the foyer of the Savoy Hotel in London. As Champion ate from the hotel's finest china, Autry must have smiled to himself and thought, "It's a long way from Tioga, Texas." Through dime novels and turn-of-the-century literature, through silent cinema, and the folk roots and commercial exploitation of cowboy songs, the historical route that ends with the horse operas of the 1930s is no less strange than that a blues-yodeling son of a Texas farmer would become one of Hollywood's biggest box-office attractions.

ONE

*By the Costume We May Tell the
Man: Turn-of-the-Century Fiction
and the Figure of the Cowboy*

"The West was suddenly a subject in 1891," wrote Thomas Beer in his
1926 account of American arts and life during the last decade of the
1800s. "The *Century* brought out notes on primitive California and a
[another] tale. . . . Careful reports of Western States and cities appeared in *Harper's*. Frederick [*sic*] Remington's sketches and the first
of Owen Wister's stories found attention."[1] Alongside this list of historical markers, and despite the historian Frederick Jackson Turner's
1893 declaration that the frontier period in U.S. history had ended
in 1890, 1891 is a more or less arbitrary date. A writer of short stories
and novels, informal histories, and biography, Beer was never particularly fastidious with facts if they got in the way of telling a good story.
He fabricated vast screeds of his biography of Stephen Crane, including some of Crane's best-known aphorisms, such as the thought that
War and Peace "went on and on like Texas" and that while "Robert Louis
Stevenson had passed away, he hadn't passed far enough."[2] As Beer's
arbitrary dating of the fascination with the West suggests, a discussion

of the subject has no definitive starting point. The cowboy entered the world of popular representations toward the close of the 1880s, principally as a participant in Buffalo Bill's Wild West show and in the spunoff dime novels that fictionalized some of the show's stars, such as Buck Taylor. Though cowboys had appeared in earlier dime novels, Daryl Jones, a historian of the genre, contends that Buck Taylor was the first widely popular literary cowboy. The first novel to deal with his exploits was published in 1887.[3]

Dime novels were cheap sensational fictions that sold by the thousand to an avid readership of working-class men and women. Beer mentioned Remington and Wister, who, with Theodore Roosevelt, would form what has become known as the eastern establishment; they held one claim to the cowboy. But despite the dominance of these authors in the history of the fictional cowboy (Remington wrote about the West while also painting, sketching, and sculpting it), the fictions created for the working and immigrant classes challenged the eastern establishment's peculiar notion of the figure. So did, in differing ways, the magazine fiction aimed at the new professional middle class and the work of female authors and African-American writers.

The exploits of Deadwood Dick, a series begun in 1877, popularized the frontier outlaw of the dime novel. Deadwood Dick was not a continuation of the earlier frontier Indian fighters that had characterized the format but an altogether new figure who, the western scholar Richard Slotkin argues, stood in opposition to the moral values held by fictional frontiersmen based on the model of James Fenimore Cooper's characters.[4] The cultural historian Michael Denning notes that Deadwood Dick, and his rival in dime novel popularity, Jesse James, are "less sons of Leatherstocking than sons of Molly Maguire [the clandestine Irish miners' union], less stories of the Wild West than stories of Labor and Capital."[5] Denning persuasively argues that the readership for dime novels was overwhelmingly working class and that the stories deal with working-class issues. They are fairy tale–like transformations of everyday life, where outlaws "defied the law and got away with it, escaping the moral universe of both genteel and sensational fiction."[6] Denning notes: "Never before had a Western hero openly defied the law. Never before had a Western hero reacted against social restraint so violently as to waylay stages and rob banks."[7] The outlaw and road agent clashed not with Indians but with private detectives hired by capitalists to protect their interests. The dime novel, then, as Marcus Klein has argued in another study of popular fiction at the turn of the century, needs to be understood as produced by urban writers for urban consumers: "The villains in the romance of the West were Mosensteins, not Indians or 'bad men,' or they were other foreigners, or radicals, or bankers, or Eastern politicians, or some several others who, similarly, were the natural enemies of the older and better scheme of things."[8]

The dime novel was not the whole of western fiction. In his analysis of the role in U.S. culture of turn-of-the-century magazines, Richard Ohmann considers the appeal of the short story to a different audience, a form designed to meet the needs and fantasies of a newly formed professional middle class.[9] His analysis reveals that the magazines principally carried two types of stories. One addressed a female readership with tales of romantic courtship, whereas the other appealed to a male readership through tales of adventure. Fictions set in the American West dominated the latter. Not, as Ohmann is quick to point out, the American West of the post–Civil War period but a contemporary West: "These turn-of-the-century magazines have acknowledged the closing of the frontier, and their fictional West is a part of American society. Trains go there, economic enterprise is underway, there are schools and courts of law. This is not the wilderness of Leatherstocking or Boone nor the barbarous outland of many dime novel Westerns. But relations of people to nature and to one another are more rudimentary in this newly tamed West than back East."[10]

Central to Ohmann's argument is the effacement of class politics in these stories: "There are no social conflicts at all, of a structural sort. No class antagonisms, no rebellious cowboys, no uprising of 'Greasers,' not even in these stories—traditional struggles between cowmen and homesteaders."[11] Ohmann's analysis of these westerns, like Denning's account of dime novels, is revelatory, but both writers make too little of their findings with regard to wider debates on the western. Denning argues that the dime novel was always class conscious and spoke, albeit at times indirectly, to the interests of its working-class readership. On the other hand, in the stories that Ohmann examines "the fictional society has classes, but no deep conflicts of interest or need dictate that classes must contend with one another. Strikes and labor organization are virtually absent from the social scene. Rich people do not exploit workers; they simply have money."[12] Taken together, the dime novel and popular magazine fiction reveal just how adaptable was the figure of the cowboy in meeting the demands of a diverse audience.

His appeal to yet another group, an established U.S. elite, was large-

ly the work of a small but highly influential group of high-born easterners headed by Roosevelt, Remington, and Wister. In 1896 Roosevelt
published a collection of his writings, illustrated by Remington, titled
Ranch Life and the Hunting Trail. The first part of the book redundant-
ly details the day-to-day work on Roosevelt's ranch, but within this dreary discourse lies a thorough attempt to construct the cowboy as America's Adam: "Civilization seems as remote as if we were living in an age
long past. The whole existence is patriarchal in character: it is the life
of men who live in the open, who tend their herds on horseback, who
go armed and ready to guard their lives by their own prowess, whose
wants are very simple, and who call no man master. Ranching is an
occupation like those of vigorous, primitive pastoral peoples, having
little in common with the humdrum, workaday business world of the
nineteenth century."[13]

Once past the self-aggrandizement in Roosevelt's writing, it becomes
apparent that his project is to establish an American identity, formed
against the combined onslaught of industrialization, urbanization, fem-
inization, and immigration. For Roosevelt ranching is a romantic idyll
colored by a Protestant work ethic and pragmatism. In this world the
Anglo-Saxon cowboy is master of all he surveys, yet he understands the
value of work, however meager the monetary rewards. He respects authority, though authority is not a right of birth but must be earned: "The
captain of the round-up, or the foreman of a wagon may himself be a
ranch man; if such is not the case, and the ranch man nevertheless
comes along, he works and fares precisely as do the other cowboys."[14]

Roosevelt's rancher is not a captain of industry, divorced from the
processes of production, but a worker alongside other workers. And
his workers are not peasants but primitives in the romantic sense that
they live outside a rigorously defined class system with its attendant
social mores and moral values: "He was a pleasant companion and
useful assistant, being very hard-working, and possessing a temper that
never was ruffled by anything. He was a good looking fellow, with honest brown eyes; but he no more knew the difference between right and
wrong than Adam did before the fall."[15]

For Roosevelt the West reveals the masculine in men, leaves wom-
en drained of bourgeois notions of femininity, and, above all, presents
a space where the inherent superiority of the Anglo-Saxon American
goes unquestioned. This may reveal itself in the simple pastime of
horse racing: "Indians and whites often race against each other as well
as among themselves. I have seen several such contests, and in every

case but one the white man happened to win."[16] The Anglo's strength of character also reveals his superiority: "Some of the cowboys are Mexicans, who generally do the actual work well enough, but are not trustworthy. . . . One spring I had with my wagon a Pueblo Indian, an excellent rider and roper, but a drunken, worthless, lazy devil."[17] Though Roosevelt accepts that the United States is a country peopled by immigrants, only those of northern European ancestry are worthy of an American identity: "It would be impossible to imagine a more typically American assemblage, for although there are always a certain number of foreigners, usually English, Irish, or German, yet they have become completely Americanized."[18]

In his comparative analysis of the frontier theses of Frederick Jackson Turner and Roosevelt, Richard Slotkin considers Roosevelt's West as a variant on the frontier, a site of "regeneration through regression." The frontier is a liminal space where a return to a more primitive state helps in the process of purifying and revitalizing an overcultivated secular soul. Through Roosevelt's discourse on Anglo-Saxon racial supremacy, Slotkin argues that Roosevelt's project is addressed not to the nation as a whole but to the captains of industry. His fear is that the leaders of the nation have become complacent and that the terror of the mob awaits those who are not willing to learn the lessons offered by the frontier experience, where a "strenuous life" proved the testing ground for Roosevelt's thesis on class and race.[19]

Roosevelt helped to elevate the cowboy from the realm of mass popular culture, giving the figure a social and cultural respectability that allowed the cowboy to be held up as the ideal American. The rapidity with which the ideas of the eastern establishment entered into wider usage can be measured by their assimilation into the writings of Emerson Hough, author of *The Story of the Cowboy* (1897).

This elegiac history begins in the studio of a western artist (perhaps Remington) whose pastime is to entertain guests by turning the studio into Plato's cave. Upon the wall are cast the shadows of his bronze and clay sculptures.

> "Look!" said he. There upon the wall, of the size of life, jaunty, erect, was the virile figure of a mounted man. He stood straight in the stirrups of his heavy saddle, but lightly and well poised. A coil of rope hung at his saddlebow. A loose belt swung a revolver low upon his hip. A wide hat blew up and back a bit with the air of his traveling, and a deep kerchief fluttered at his neck. His arm, held lax and high, offered sup-

port to the slack reins so little needed in his riding. The small and sinewy steed beneath him was alert and vigorous as he. It was a figure vivid, keen, remarkable. When it vanished there was silence, for perhaps here were those who thought upon the story that had been told.[20]

Recalled through shadow play and storytelling, the cowboy has passed into history. The story told by Hough—long winded, endlessly repetitive—is that "the American cowboy is the most gallant modern representative of human industry second to very few in antiquity. I use the present tense, but . . . the cowboy is already receding into the shadows of the past years." This is from the editor's preface, but it serves as a summation of Hough's thesis. The cowboy is a modern figure, yet he resembles heroic figures from antiquity. He is of the present but is slipping into the past.

As with Roosevelt's West, Hough imagines a classless society; the rangeland is owned by "kings who paid no tribute, and guarded by men who never knew a master."[21] Yet Hough's story is concerned with mapping a vast industry. It is a celebration of capital, and despite his claims to the contrary, the cowboys are employees who are dependent on the largesse of their bosses. Hough offers the life of the cowboy as a corrective to a comfortable, sterile, corporate existence, where success has led to "more and more wealth, more and more artificiality, more and more degeneration."[22] Where life has become a meaningless round of fads and fashions, "by the costume we may tell the man. We can not fail to recognize a nature [the cowboy's] vigorous far beyond those weak degenerates who study constantly upon changes in their own bedeckings."[23] Hough continues: "Let us not ask whence the cowboy came, for that is a question immaterial and impossible to answer. Be sure, he came from among those who had strong within them the savagery and love of freedom which springs so swiftly into life among strong natures when offered a brief exemption from the slavery of civilization."[24] This reworking of Roosevelt's ideas about a "strenuous life" inevitably leads to the celebration of patriarchal Anglo-Saxon American supremacy. Hough continued these themes in his later fiction, notably with *The Covered Wagon* (1922) and *North of 36* (1923).

Unlike the authors of dime novels and popular magazine fiction, who set their stories in the present, the eastern elite set their tales of the West firmly in the past. In "The Evolution of the Cow-Puncher" (1895), an essay written in consultation with Remington and published in *Harper's,* Wister introduced the model for the character of the cowboy hero in *The Virginian* (1902). His project was to reconcile the character traits of the English aristocrat and the self-made American—in effect bridging the distinction between high brow and low brow. To this end he has an English peer fall upon hard times. The peer moves to Texas, where, we learn, "the slumbering untamed Saxon awoke in him."[25] The nobleman is "fundamentally kin with the drifting vagabonds who swore and galloped by his side."[26] Who were these vagabonds? Like Roosevelt and Hough, Wister ignores the historical reality of an ethnically heterogeneous group of men who worked as cowboys in the Southwest and suppresses the presence of African Americans and people of other races: "To survive in the clean cattle country requires spirit of adventure, courage and self-sufficiency; you will not find many Poles or Huns or Russian Jews in that district."[27]

Wister contrasts the "cleanliness" of the West to the "filth" of the city, "with its hordes of encroaching alien vermin, that turn our cities to Babels and our citizenship to a hybrid farce."[28] It is important for Wister to stress the similarities between the cowboy and the aristocrat, and the continuity that lies between them, "from Camelot to the round-up at Abilene," because he wishes to efface the role of class in establishing an American identity and yet to maintain his claim to belong to an American elite.[29]

If outlaw and cowboy of the dime novel were figures who sided with the needs and desires of labor, Roosevelt's, Wister's, and Remington's westerners were aligned with the interests of capital. The fear of organized labor is implicit in *The Virginian*, but letters and journalism give that fear an explicit airing. In his sketches and report of the Chicago riots of 1894, Remington placed the Seventh Cavalry ("just come from Indian fighting") as a bulwark between "real Americans" and "the rats."[30]

Race clearly has an unequivocal role, as the discourse of white supremacism divides Wister's cowboys from the unruly mob. Nonetheless, the cowboys need some hierarchy that is not based on traditional class divisions and is not an affront to the principles of the Declaration of Independence, which declared all men as equal. Wister's answer is to propose a distinction between "equality" and "quality." Slotkin argues that Wister is able to claim that "certain forms of democracy produce a degenerate form of politics: one in which mongrels and failures, the 'equality,' are enabled to assert against the 'quality' their claims for power and a redistribution of wealth."[31] Wister repositions the class struggle as being between a "true aristocracy" and a "false democracy." His representative cowboy is therefore both democrat and aristocrat, a fictional resolving of clearly contradictory positions. By making historical claims for the veracity of his representation, Wister hopes to efface the contradiction.

The mythification that Roosevelt, Remington, and Wister carried out was not the only way of looking at the recent history of the West. Another, very different approach appears in the writings of Frank Norris, who argued that dime novel and Wild West representations had so degraded the figure of the cowboy as to make him no longer suitable material in any meaningful account of U.S. history: "We had the material, Homer found no better, the heroes, the great fights, the play of unleashed, unfettered passionate humanity, and we let it all go, this national epic of America, the only one we shall ever have, to the wretched 'Deadwood Dicks' and Buffalo Bills of the yellow backs."[32]

Norris figures large in *The Mauve Decade,* Beer's chronicle of this crucial epoch in the formation of the cowboy. Following an impressionistic account of the demise of the Dalton Gang, the last of the "mannerly bandits," Beer turns away from the mythological exploits of western bad men and focuses his story of the turn-of-the-century West upon the rise of the Populists and, most particularly, the rise of the robber barons in the guise of the Southern Pacific Railroad. Beer interlaces his narrative with accounts of the Pullman and other strikes, of Coxey's Army of tramps heading toward Washington, D.C., in 1894, and ends with the novelist Frank Norris strolling through his beloved San Francisco streets.

Beer assigned his merrily vituperative western "history" to a chapter called "Wasted Land," where he mocks the idea of the West as "virgin land." Echoing the poet in Norris's *The Octopus* (1901), Beer appears to be calling for a "Song of the West," an American epic to match those of the Old World. But like Norris's poet, Beer finds only sordid deeds. Norris's poet imagines a romance that would catch forever the heroic endeavors of the westerner, but the banalities of everyday life repeatedly undermine him:

> He had set himself the task of giving true, absolutely true, poetical expression to the life of the ranch, and yet, again and again, he brought up against the railroad, that stubborn iron barrier against which his romance shattered itself to froth and disintegrated, flying spume. His heart went out to the people, and his groping hand met that of a slovenly little Dutchman, whom it was impossible to consider seriously. He

searched for the True Romance, and in the end, found grain rates and unjust freight tariffs.[33]

The Octopus is a fictionalized account of the 1880 Mussel Slough massacre, where California farmers in the San Joaquin valley fought a fearsome gun battle with railroad representatives. As the historian Richard Maxwell Brown notes, the massacre did not find a place in the mythology of the American West alongside more notorious events, such as the shoot-out at the OK Corral.[34] The myth of the OK Corral effaces the political conflict that led to the gunfight. The Mussel Slough massacre was nothing but politics—ranchers and farmers against a railroad monopoly backed by the government. Norris's decision to rework the Mussel Slough massacre as fiction suggests both a desire for novelty and a rejection of many tenets of the frontier myth.

In "The Literature of the West" (1902), which he wrote a year after the publication of *The Octopus,* Norris mourned the loss of the opportunity to write "The Epic of the West." This was a story that had been despoiled by the "traducing, falsifying dime novels which have succeeded only in discrediting our one great chance for distinctive American literature."[35] Dime novels, he contended, had reduced the characterization of the West to the miner and the cowboy, with "his stock lingo, his makeup, his swagger and his gallery plays. . . . He was a characteristic once, but now he is only a very bad actor who dresses the part according to the illustrated weeklies, and who, 'pour épater les bourgeois,' wears 'chaps' on the plains."[36] In "The Frontier Gone at Last," another essay published in the same year, Norris argues that the story of the Anglo-Saxon's "Westward progress" did not end with the closing of the American frontier but continues in the realm of trade, with the winning of markets in Asia. This was a theme he worked into his proposed trilogy, beginning with *The Octopus,* which examined the production, distribution, and consumption of wheat.

Despite the apparent hollowness of the cowboy's representation in dime novels and Norris's claim for an epic vision of U.S. history and progress that ignored the dominant conception of westward expansion, the cowboy still found a space in his fiction. In *The Octopus* the braggart Delaney "plays" the cowboy":

> Delaney had arrayed himself with painful elaboration, determined to look the part, bent upon creating the impression, resolved that his appearance at least should justify his reputation of being "bad." Noth-

ing was lacking—neither the campaign hat with up-turned brim, nor the dotted blue handkerchief knotted behind the neck, nor the heavy gauntlets stitched with red, nor—this above all—the bear-skin "cha-parejos," the hair trousers of the mountain cowboy, the pistol holster low on the thigh. But for the moment the holster was empty, and in his right hand, the hammer at full cock, the chamber loaded, the puncher flourished his teaser, an army Colt's, the lamp-light dully reflected in the dark blue steel.[37]

Delaney is, literally and figuratively, an actor. He will play his part as stooge for the railroad in the cataclysmic shoot-out at the novel's end; in this passage, costumed and masquerading as a bad man, he plays a role that first appeared in the pages of a Deadwood Dick dime novel. There is something ridiculous about Norris's cowboys, as though he recognized their iconographic importance within stories of the West but cannot overcome their lowly degraded status as dime novel characters.

In *McTeague* (1899), Norris's masterpiece of American naturalism, a character fancies a life away from the squalor of San Francisco's Polk Street and brags of getting into "ranching" with an English gent. Nor-ris gives his consent to this fancy: "His life was the life of a cowboy. He realized his former vision of himself, booted, sombreroed, and revolv-ered, passing his days in the saddle and the better parts of his nights around the poker tables in Modoc's one saloon. To his intense satis-faction he even involved himself in a gun fight that arose over a dis-puted brand, with the result that two fingers of his left hand were shot away."[38] By the time Norris had begun his career as an essayist and novelist in the 1890s, the figure of the cowboy had risen from its ob-scure origins as a proletarian agricultural worker to become a signifi-cant character in the fictions that accompanied the development of the mass culture of the United States. Norris's cowboys carry the signs of this fictive status: the costume, the saloon, card playing, and gunfights about cattle. Norris's fictions mark the cowboy's image as an already mediated representation, lacking in the verities necessary to create an American hero: "Once or twice cowboys passed them on the road, big-boned fellows, picturesque in their broad hats, hairy trousers, jingling spurs, and revolver belts, surprisingly like the pictures Mc-Teague remembered to have seen."[39] A product of the city, McTeague mentally filters his encounters with the "real" through the represen-tations he has previously experienced. This motif is also present in some of Stephen Crane's western stories. In *The Blue Hotel* (1898) three travelers—a Swede, an easterner, and a cowboy—take respite in a Nebraska hotel. During a friendly game of cards the Swede becomes increasingly paranoid and accuses the others of wanting to kill him. The easterner tries to explain the Swede's irrational actions: "It seems to me this man has been reading dime-novels, and he thinks he's right out in the middle of it—the shootin' and the stabbin' and all. 'But,' said the cowboy, deeply scandalized, 'this ain't Wyoming, ner none of them places. This is Nebrasker.' "[40] Whatever the reality, by the turn-of-the-century the cowboy was a wholly fictional figure.

In *Trickster in the Land of Dreams* the historian Zeese Papanikolas offers an alternative and conflicting version of the West to the myth of the noble cowboy found in the work of Roosevelt, Remington, and Wister. In a chapter titled "Cowboys, Wobblies, and the Myth of the West," Papanikolas argues that the myth functions as a "tool for the distortion of historical reality, [which] was paid for by the laboring men and women whose lives and struggles it attempted to devalue or deny." He considers Roosevelt and company's version of the West against the countermyth produced by the Industrial Workers of the World, a "myth of the western worker that matched and opposed [the eastern establishment's] view of human possibility."[41] Thus, despite the elite's appropriation of the cowboy as an agent of patriarchal Anglo-Saxon supremacism and class hierarchy, the figure still held great appeal to the men and women who were excluded from an active participation in a republic visualized and governed by such personages as Roosevelt.

Narratives produced by African-American cowboys also stressed an anxiety about their place in the republic that they addressed in terms of class rather than racial politics. Identifying with the preeminent American outlaw, Jesse James, both Nat Love and James Cape claimed to have been his friend. Recalling only that working for the James brothers was a noteworthy event in his long life, Cape leaves open the question of their outlawry.[42] On the other hand, Love creates a link between the James Gang and the robber barons: "By what name are we to call some of the great trusts, corporations and brokers, who have for years been robbing the people of this country? . . . The only difference between them and the James brothers is that the James brothers stole from the rich and gave to the poor, while these respected members of society steal from the poor to make the rich richer."[43] This was a critique of robber barons and a defense of outlawry familiar to dime novels. As Daryl Jones notes, one function of the dime novel outlaw was to "point out the iniquity of a social system that sanctions the exploitation of the common man by an unscrupulous ruling class."[44]

The appeal of the figure of the cowboy crossed not only class but gender lines. In *West of Everything* Jane Tompkins persuasively argues that the western appeared as a patriarchal response to the culture upheld in the domestic, sentimental, nineteenth-century novel: "The Western *answers* the domestic novel. It is the antithesis of the cult of domesticity that dominated American Victorian culture. The Western hero, who seems to ride in out of nowhere, in fact comes riding in out of the nineteenth century. . . . Repeating the pattern of the domestic novels in reverse, Westerns either push women out of the picture completely or assign them roles in which they exist only to serve the needs of men."[45] However, Tompkins bases her argument on a limited number of novels and films: Wister's *Virginian,* Grey's *Riders of the Purple Sage,* works of Louis L'Amour, and a highly selective list from the canon of post–World War II auteurist westerns. Though her argument is essentially historical, the evidence she provides is resolutely ahistorical, taking no account of earlier manifestations that contest the masculinist version of the western that she produces. Tompkins ignores dime novels and popular magazine fiction of the turn of the century and the first forty-odd years of the film western. She also fails to recognize female writers such as B. M. Bower and Edna Ferber, whose contributions to western fiction challenge the assumptions that Tompkins labors under.[46]

In his discussion of late nineteenth-century western dime novels, Klein notes: "With considerable frequency, women were the protagonists of these fictions, and were in fact the more likely to be cast into roles of general retaliation just because they were the more likely to have suffered from the degradation of the true law."[47] Denning too notes that the representation of working-class womanhood in dime novels stressed "physical action and violence." He continues: "Just as the outlaw flourished more in the mining camps of Leadville [the setting for Deadwood Dick stories] than in those of Pottsville [the setting for Molly Maguire stories], so a physically active, non-genteel woman flourished more in the streets of Deadwood than in those of New York. . . . The heroines of the cheap stories skirt the boundaries of genteel codes."[48] Indeed; and women "skirt" this most effectively in the fiction of Bertha Muzzy Bower, the best-selling author of *Chip of the Flying U* (1904). Discussing the difference in the gender address of *The Virginian* and Bower's work, Mary Clearman Blew suggests that women too like looking at cowboys, but if, like Bower, she were going to fantasize about one she liked, it would not be the Virginian, "who would bore any girl with his rhapsodizing and drive her wild with his moralizing and his insistence on having his own way."[49] Bower's stories of cowboys and ranch life do not have the requisite climactic gunfights and exclusive focus on the male domain that are so much a part of received histories of the genre. Yet Bower's work was phenomenally successful, easily the equal of Wister's in terms of sales. Her first novel would be filmed four times and another thirteen of her novels would be adapted for the screen before 1929.

Written to appeal to both male and female sensibilities, Bower's stories of the Flying U Ranch are essentially concerned with the domestic sphere, emphasizing courtship and comedy over action and violence. As Blew argues, Bower's first novel can be read as a western woman's answer to the masculine hyperbole of *The Virginian*. The story concerns the courtship between Chip, a ranch hand with a knowledge of Shakespeare, and the Little Doctor, a younger sister of the "Old Man," who owns the ranch. The Little Doctor's imminent arrival creates all kinds of speculation as to what sort of woman the denizens of the ranch can expect from this stranger. They attempt to fit her into the usual female stereotypes, but the Little Doctor soon disabuses them of their prejudices. Chip's infatuation grows steadily through the course of story but is complicated by the Little Doctor's constant references to Dr. Cecil Granthum, whom Chip believes is a rival for her affections. Bower builds up Chip's frustration, climaxing at the end when he finally meets Dr. Granthum—a veiled parody of the showdown that ends *The Virginian*. The sense of expectation linked to this confrontation becomes palpable, even though the reader understands that Chip and the Little Doctor will form the inevitable couple and, that despite Chip's anxiety, Granthum will probably turn out to be an old man and merely a friend and benefactor to the Little Doctor. Bower, however, turns this expectation on its head. In an echo of his first meeting with the Little Doctor, Chip is assigned to meet Granthum's train, and he feels as if he is facing the gallows. Bower tortuously delays the final encounter, and Chip's imagination runs wild, but his expectations, like the reader's, are rent asunder:

> Dr. Cecil advanced with hand out invitingly. "I've heard so much about Chip that I feel very well acquainted. I hope you won't want me to call you Mr. Bennett, for I shan't, you know."

Too utterly at sea to make a reply, Chip took the offered hand in his. Hate Dr. Cecil? How could he hate this big, breezy, blue-eyed young woman? She shook his hand heartily and smiled deep into his troubled eyes, and drew the poison from his wounds in one glance.[50]

The domestic emphasis of the novels is neatly encapsulated in the idea of the ranch hands' forming a "happy family." Bower carries characters forward from one story to the next, which maintains continuity and allows her the space to develop their individual traits. In *The Happy Family of the Flying U* (1907), Chip drops into the background and Andy Green—a skilled horseman and an incorrigible teller of tall tales—takes the lead. The novel begins with the happy family grouped around a campfire with Andy spinning a story. The scene ends in gunfire, however. The main thrust of the story is Andy's courtship of a young stenographer from San Jose. As Andy mentally itemizes her attractions—her "fluffy pompadour," "sleeves that came no further than the elbow and heels higher than any riding boot Andy ever owned in his life," her white teeth that showed a "glint of gold here and there," and "finger nails that shone"—he wonders whether she has those "housewifely accomplishments that make a man dream of a little home for two."[51] This is a daydream that would never cross the stunted imaginations of the western heroes whom Tompkins dissects. Characterized as modern through her disruption of traditional gender roles, the Little Doctor proves to be a worthy match for a cowboy. For all her modernity the stenographer, however, is shown not to be worthy of the love of a cowboy. The modernity that she represents is superficial, like her mode of dress, and inauthentic, like her teeth and fingernails. "So far as Andy could see, her knowledge of cooking extended no farther than rolled oat porridge." Here Bower is not simply reinscribing fixed gender positions. Rather her concern is with establishing an idea of companionship in which both male and female have an equal commitment—it is the cowboy who "dreams of a little home for two," not the woman.

In *Lonesome Land* (1912) Bower turns away from the broad comedy and local intrigues of the happy family dramas. In this novel the "dream home" becomes a prison fashioned in hell for the wife of a rancher. The West that seems to offer immense possibilities to the inhabitants of the Flying U Ranch here becomes a land of stalled ambition and, despite the landscape, limited horizons for its denizens. The heroine has married an abusive alcoholic, and romantic notions of

domestic bliss soon turn to terror as she is left alone to face the elements. However, with inner resolve and the friendship of a cowpuncher
she begins to fight back. Toward the end of the novel she visits Arline,
from whom she hopes to borrow money: "It has come to that. I can't
remain here and keep any shred of self-respect. All my life I've been
taught to believe divorce a terrible thing—a crime, almost; now I think
it is a crime *not* to be divorced." Arline's response is equally forthright:
"I ain't sayin' they're all of 'em bad—I c'n afford to give the devil his
due and still say men is the limit. The good ones is so durn scarce it
ain't one woman in fifty lucky enough to git one. All I blame you for is
stayin' with him as long as you have. I'd of quit long ago; I was begin-
nin' to think you never would come to your senses. But you had to fight
that thing out for yourself; every woman has to."[52] In the end events
make the divorce unnecessary, but the heroine's intent is unambiguous, and, as Pam Houston notes in her introduction to a 1997 reprint
of the novel, it is not the cowpuncher or any other man who saves her.[53]

The assertion of female independence carries over in a much more
suggestive manner in Bower's Flying U Ranch stories, and she is best
remembered for these. In their representation of a western world that
is at once isolated from, yet open to, the modern world, in their emphasis on domestic and companionate relationships, with their love
of horsemanship and the characters' easy movement through and
across landscapes, and in their broad use of comedy, these stories fore-
shadow the singing westerns of the 1930s. Except as a counter to the
West offered by Wister, Bower's stories have little in common with her
more acclaimed peer.

What unites all the various constructions of the cowboy addressed
here is his formulation as a site of spectacle—an object to be gazed
upon and admired. The meaning of the cowboy shifts, depending on
the position of the producer and receiver of the image, who are not
necessarily complementary, as Beer reveals in his discussion of *The
Virginian*. Wister lived to see the cowboy become the preeminent
American symbol in the twentieth century, but he must have been dis-
mayed at how his beloved character fully failed to escape his "tawdry"
dime novel origins and how *The Virginian* would be reclaimed as a hero
by those whom Wister most despised. Near the conclusion of *The Mauve
Decade* Beer notes that *The Virginian* was a story "popular among the
plebs." He recalls an anecdote about a surgeon tending the injuries
of a soldier during the Great War; he "saw that the fellow had *The Virginian* beside the pillow and asked what he found in the story. 'Why,'

said the unsophisticated creature . . . 'this cowboy in the book, he's alive from the waist down.'"[54]

As the narrator of *The Virginian* enters the town of Medicine Bow, he looks out through a Pullman car window. He notices a man sitting on the gate of a corral and begins a description of this cowboy that confirms the wounded soldier's reading of the Virginian: "He now climbed down with the undulations of a tiger, smooth and easy, as if his muscles flowed beneath his skin. . . . He appeared to hold the rope down low, by his leg. But like a sudden snake I saw the noose go out its length and fall true; and the thing was done." A page or two later the Virginian is "lounging there at ease against the wall . . . a slim young giant, more beautiful than pictures." The narrator imagines himself as a woman: "Had I been the bride, I should have taken the giant, dust and all."[55] The sexualization of the cowboy was already present in Wister's original essay, "The Evolution of the Cow-Puncher." In a long paragraph that begins with his imagining a cowboy's flesh being torn to ribbons by the "blades and points" of chaparral and cacti, Wister offers an eroticized description of the cowboy's accoutrements and clothing: "But he cases his leg against the hostile *chaparral* from thigh to ankle in chaps—leathern breeches, next door to armor. . . . Soon his barbaric pleasure in finery sews tough leather fringe along their sides, and the leather flap of the pocket becomes stamped with a heavy rose. Sagging in a slant upon his hips leans his leather belt of cartridges buckled with jaunty arrogance, and though he uses his pistol with murderous skill, it is pretty, with ivory or mother-of-pearl for a handle."[56] Despite the use of "masculine" adjectives—*barbaric, tough, heavy*—the description feminizes the cowboy, an object of the gaze, caught and held for the viewer's pleasure. Wister was not alone in this "vision" of the cowboy; most turn-of-the-century stories of the West use this motif. Norris's descriptions are another example. Stephen Crane, in his short story "Twelve O'Clock" (1899), offers this version: "A six-shooter swung low on his hip, but at the moment it looked more decorative than warlike; it seemed merely a part of his odd gala dress—his sombrero with its band of rattlesnake skin, his great flaming neckerchief, his belt of embroidered Mexican leather, his high-heeled boots, his huge spurs. And, above all, his hair had been watered and brushed until it lay as close to his head as the fur lays to a wet cat."[57] The fascination with the "look" at (and of) the cowboy is a motif that transcends the various western narratives at turn of the century. The dime novel hero Denver Dan (a miner by day and a vigilante by night) is introduced as the finest of specimens: "A nearer view of the solitary rider would have shown that he was not only well mounted, but well armed, also; and that upon his face was a half mask of black silk, and around his throat was a silken cord, to which was attached a silver whistle, now concealed in the bosom of his richly-ornamented shirt."[58] But next to his rival dime-novel character, Dandy Dan of Deadwood, Denver Dan appears rather dreary. Daryl Jones has called Dandy Dan the "ultimate in fop heroes." He wears a "suit of neat black velvet, with patent leather boots on his feet. He wore a white shirt, the front of which was spotless, and in the center of the bosom blazed a magnificent diamond. His broad-brimmed sombrero at his side was gathered up at one corner by a rich cluster of diamonds."[59] As Jones points out, the costume bares the traces of the stage and Wild West shows rather than the cattle trail. But whatever their provenance, flamboyant costumes worn by cowboys such as Dandy Dan counter the idea of the capitalist villain's cutting a more dashing figure than the working-class hero.

If the privileging or effacement of class struggle defines their differences, the cowboy as spectacle unites the versions. And not only those narratives that are class distinct but also stories that are gender specific in their address: "The tall young fellow in fringed leather chaps and big rowelled silver spurs stood still as carved granite beside the kitchen table. A holstered six-shooter hung snug at his right hip in odd contrast to the checked gingham apron tied around his neck."[60] This is from a short story by Bower. She would incorporate the filming of westerns in her stories, whereas Wister saw the movies in a very different light. In an anti-immigration tirade, "Shall We Let the Cuckoos Crowd Us out of Our Nest?" (1921), he wrote: "Cuckoos there are who would like to change New York's name to Moscow and call Broadway Lenine [*sic*] Street; other cuckoos would rename Washington, Dublin. And we have opened our doors to these birds, made them welcome!" He finishes with stern advice: "Eternal vigilance cannot watch Liberty and the movies at the same time."[61]

The movies would continue the tradition of contesting claims regarding the figure of the cowboy. However, during the formative years of the U.S. film industry (1907–14), the issue of the cowboy's class allegiance would be particularly pronounced, and the nature of the figure of the cowboy as a site of spectacle would be reworked.

TWO

Liberty's Cuckoos: Cowboys of the Silent Screen

To what extent do the literary versions help form the image of the cowboy as he appears in the early silent cinema? In *Westerns: Making the Man in Fiction and Film* (1997), Lee Clark Mitchell depicts the cowboy as a mythic unchanging figure whose lineage reaches back across nine decades to the hero of Owen Wister's *The Virginian:* "The image remains the same in countless versions—a lone man packing a gun, astride a horse, hat pulled close to the eyes, emerging as if by magic out of an empty landscape."[1] Mitchell's conception confirms both scholarly and popular formulations of the western, which see the figure of the cowboy as a historically immutable character; "Wister's novel became the paradigm text of the Western film genre," writes Slotkin.[2] But regardless of its critical currency, *The Virginian* is not the Ur-text of the film western. The early film cowboy is a dowdy, unglamorous, and often horseless protagonist who bears little resemblance to either Mitchell's "Lone Man" or Wister's "Horseman of the Plains." He is more likely to be standing in front of a clapboard building than emerging from a limitless horizon. Most probably, his hat will be a well-worn, sometimes shapeless, affair matched by the rest of an ill-fitting costume that symbolizes not mystery and resoluteness but utility and function. His gun, neckerchief, leather gauntlets, and chaps remain an important focus of his appeal, yet the overarching visual stylization of the figure of the cowboy as a *worker* alters the appeal of the spectacle as performed by figures such as the Virginian. What differentiates the cowboy of the early silent film era (1907–14) from its turn-of-the-century written fictional antecedents is the shift from the figure of the cowboy as a spectacle of description to a spectacle of action. This shift to a narrative of performance typifies the film form and further furnishes popular images of the working-class cowboy. The actor G. M. Anderson's popular character, Broncho Billy, is particularly representative of the worker-cowboy in early film westerns. Anderson presented a stocky, almost portly, figure with a bulbous nose. In looks and deportment he would have made a poor model for the statuesque hero whose lineage Wister traced to the knights of the Round Table.[3] The characters played by Anderson suggest no such grandiose bloodlines. The single-reel early western film narratives forsook the qualities of the epic and concentrated instead on dramas of intrigue, on small localized disputes and conflicts. These tend not to represent national foundation stories of progress and westward migration but a fairly static view of rural life enlivened by threats to property or person.

In his study of working-class films Steven J. Ross notes that at "no time in the industry's history would filmmakers be more concerned with the lives and hardships of working people than during the Progressive era."[4] As Ross points out, this is not particularly remarkable when film's principal audience from 1900 to 1920 was overwhelmingly urban and working class. In 1910 westerns represented 21 percent of the films produced in United States. Ross cites only two examples of westerns that dealt with the conflict between capital and labor: *The Agitator* (Triangle, 1912) and *The Strike at the "Little Jonny" Mine* (Essanay, 1911), both starring "Broncho Billy" Anderson.[5] But many pre-1920s westerns are concerned with class struggle, at least implicitly.

Michael Denning, along with Richard Ohmann, Zeese Papanikolas, and Marcus Klein, offers the possibility of imagining a West that is separate from the frontier myth. These writers share a view of the genre as an overt engagement with modernization and modernity. An obscure single-reel film, *Cowboys' Day Off* (Broncho Films, 1912), exemplifies the continuation of this process of engagement through film

Charles M. Russell's
pen drawing of "The
Virginian," the first
representation of
Owen Wister's hero.
(Ammon Carter Muse-
um, Ft. Worth, Tex.)

during the first decades of the twentieth century; it offers the unusual
conceit of cowboys on Coney Island.

By taking cowboys out of the West, *Cowboys' Day Off* has the effect
of magnifying, and bringing into relief, the differences between Wister's knightly cowboy and early films' worker cowboys. The film's novelty is the idea of the rural and apparently premodern cowboy con-
fronting the urban and modern attractions of Coney Island.[6] Unlike
the rural figure of the rube—a familiar character in films from this
period—the cowboys are not overwhelmed by the city's attractions.
Instead, they show themselves to be its master—actively courting

Broncho Billy Anderson (*left*) in a typical barroom scene, this one from *Broncho Billy's Double Escape* (1914). Note how stocky he appears compared to Russell's Virginian.

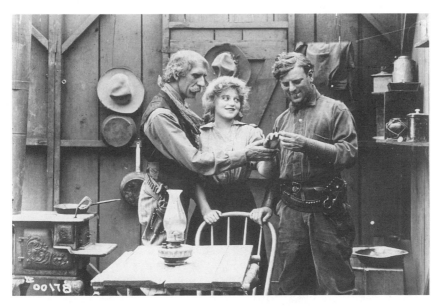

Broncho Billy Anderson (*right*) in a typical domestic scene, this one from *Broncho Billy's Oath*, placing a wedding ring on the heroine's finger.

sensation.[7] Rather than the city overwhelming the cowboys, the cowboys, literally and figuratively, overwhelm the city.

The film begins with the cowboys collecting their pay and then commandeering a car. They drive to the railroad depot, where they board a train. During the journey east they indulge in drinking and tomfoolery, much of it at the expense of a black car attendant. Before they throw him off the moving train, the cowboys make the attendant dance by shooting bullets into the floor around his nimble feet. On arrival at Coney Island the cowboys pick up women and then ride on the fairground attractions. In between they lasso alligators and ride on the backs of ostriches. In a parallel story line a fellow train traveler is pursued through Coney Island by his umbrella-wielding wife. The film ends the following morning, back at the ranch, with the cowboys paying for their day of fun and laughter with hangovers.

Though none of the cowboys is individuated, the opening of the film takes time to establish the cowboys as the principal protagonists, which encourages audience identification with the film's theme—the consumption of leisure (signaled by the title and confirmed by the first intertitle, "Pay Day at the Ranch"). The cowboys spend their pay on ephemeral and sensory products—travel, alcohol, and fairground rides—equivalent to the film audience spending its money on cinema tickets.

The second scene establishes a contemporary setting and the cowboys' ability to master the preeminent symbol of modernity, the automobile. Their fooling around in a car sets up the film's comic credentials, formed around the idea of a male group let loose from the responsibilities of work. In the third scene, aboard the train, the cowboys partake in a round of social and public drinking. While some passengers shy away from the cowboys' antics, others join in, particularly the man with a fusty wife.

The cowboys' pleasures are simple, sensory, immediate, and unhampered by any permanently debilitating attachment to women, evidently a contrast to the husband, who is offered as an alternative to the cowboys of a rural premodernity. The cowboys will suffer only the punishment of hangovers for their day of leisure and excess, but this man will suffer his wife's constant harassment and regulation.

Coney Island offers the spectacle and thrills of its amusements as a substitute for the western landscape that had become, by 1910, a cornerstone of the industry's marketing of the genre.[8] Similarly, the cowboys are posed as physical spectacle: they pit their skills against exotic animals, which comically replace the horse and the steer, encouraging the view of their cavorting and roistering as an added attraction for Coney Island's pleasure seekers. The cowboys present themselves as performers for an urban audience, an image that supports Marcus Klein's argument that the genre needs to be understood as being produced by urban easterners for urban easterners. Klein was describing the literary western, but his argument also holds true for many early film westerns.

If *Cowboys' Day Off* is an anomaly in its use of an eastern locale, it nevertheless shared a modern setting with a number of other westerns of the period. The automobile is a fairly familiar prop. For example, in *The Distant Relative* (American, 1912) the plot is resolved when the cowboys swap their horses for a car to overtake a horse-drawn buggy more quickly. Clearly, not all early westerns have contemporary settings, but those that do not signify any particular temporality, such as *The Mexican's Faith* (Essanay, 1910), could just as easily be set in the present as in the past. The use of Indians most often signifies that a western is historical, but even in a film like *The Frenzy of Fire-Water* (Kalem, 1912), which features a dramatic scene of Indians circling a wagon train, the tendency is to highlight contemporary concerns, in this case the effects of alcohol abuse, rather than those of the Old West. Moreover, not all the films that feature Indians are set in the past. *Curse of the Redman* (Selig, 1911), another cautionary tale about the ravages of drink, has a contemporary setting, indicated by diegetic date signs and intertitles. Temperance stories were a major theme in films from this period, offering sensational subject matter with a morally uplifting message. The western also depicted other contemporary themes. Woman suffrage and, notably, the fad for white slave narratives (the white heroine's abduction and threatened seduction by the city slicker) both provided significant narrative themes for the early film western.[9]

Film after film from this period presents the cowboy as a worker, in contrast to the city slicker. When he meets the challenges presented by the city slicker, who will often work in cahoots with a Mexican or Indian, the cowboy establishes his racial, class, and rural credentials.[10] It is not commerce per se that the films hold accountable but exploitive individuals who signify the corrupting influence of the city. These films do not always view negatively interaction with the wider world of capital. In *Una of the Sierras* (Vitagraph, 1912), which has a contemporary setting, the daughter of a gold prospector successfully invests in the stock market. The plot translates her innocence of city ways into a set of moral values for which she is rewarded. In general, the cowboy's inevitable victory refuses any deference to a class hierarchy, a hierarchy further effaced by the imposition of a racial hierarchy that he, as a white man, dominates.

Westerns that show the city dweller going west and becoming a cowboy are more tales of democracy in action and less Rooseveltian stories of regeneration through strenuous activity. In *The Making of Broncho Billy* (Essanay, 1913) a tenderfoot travels west. The butt of the cowboys' jokes, he finds a place for himself in their group when he acquires the skills and dress of the cowboy. This is a story not of regeneration but of assimilation. These films offer class as the defining conflict, with the end goal defined by the hero's assimilation into a democratic group. The films achieve this result through the transformation of the urban upper-class protagonist into a rural working-class cowboy, the opposite of *The Virginian*, where the hero-cowboy becomes a successful property owner and capitalist.

In *The Corporation and the Ranch Girl* (Essanay, 1911) a playboy, on his father's orders, travels west to trick a young woman out of her ranch. Corporate greed and trickery are confounded not through contact with the wilderness but through the love of the ranch girl. The playboy rejects his father and the city and becomes an honest cowboy. In *Cowboy for Love* (Bison, 1911) a rich young man falls in love with a girl below his class. When his father refuses to give his permission for them to marry, they elope and move west. Three years pass, and the father goes in search of his son. He finds he has a grandchild and that his son is happy working as a cowboy.

The Cowboy Millionaire (Selig, 1909) parodies the romantic Wisterian view of the cowboy and reverses the process of the urbanite going west by turning a cowboy into a man of money and leisure. The film, which has a number of similarities to *Cowboys' Day Off*, opens on a ranch with a large group of cowboys displaying their roping and riding talents. One receives notice that he has been left $10 million. While in Chicago to collect his money, he falls in love and changes his cowboy costume for a tailored suit. Time passes, and he arranges for his pals to pay a visit. The cowboys create a rude interruption in the sedate middle-class life of Chicago by dominating the city streets and disrupting a theatrical show. Their return to the ranch leaves the millionaire cowboy alone in his study, surrounded by objects portraying a strenuous and sporting life imagined rather than lived: a statuette of a bucking broncho, a painting of cowboys, a swordfish spear, and various medieval knickknacks mounted around a huge fireplace.[11] He has money and a wife, but he lacks true companionship, and his links to a wider community are in the past. Instead of celebrating the eastern establishment's view of the cowboy, the film reveals its lack of authenticity. It characterizes the modern city as a world of fictions: the objects in the study, the theatrical performance of a western melodrama. As part of a theater audience, the cowboys are unable to distinguish between reality and fiction and shoot the play's villain, an act of violence against representation that asserts their authenticity.

Cowboys' Day Off shares a similar set of concerns. By taking the cowboy out of his natural environment, the film points to the division between work and the consumption of leisure. We first see the cowboys being paid for their labor and then how they spend their money. But the film then evades the issues it raises. It does this by making play out of the skills that the cowboys use in their work. With the emphasis now on their mastery of animals and objects provided by the pleasure grounds, the film transforms work into spectacle, which a willing audience (both at Coney Island and in the cinema) then consumes. The performance of the cowboys at Coney Island transcends the previously established division between work and leisure. Despite the implication established at the beginning of the film, that the cowboys are "wage slaves" rather than their own masters, the film moves the audience's attention away from this image and on to the cowboys' control of narrative events. Neither modernity, as represented by Coney Island, nor the cowboys' subservience in terms of class, is posed as a problem.

The cowboys' success in creating desire in the young women that they encounter raises and confirms their masculine potency by contrasting them with the ineffectual patriarchal figure dominated by his wife and, more pointedly, through the construction of a racial hierarchy. The central event of the train journey is the prank that the cowboys play on the black car attendant (a similar incident appears in *Cowboy Millionaire*). The black character brings the film's racism more clearly into focus than if the filmmakers had chosen to use a Native American or Mexican-American character. In early and even later westerns the ubiquitous use of negative racial stereotyping of Indians and Mexicans has the effect of dulling sensibilities and making the racist attitudes of these films less visible. The cowboys' interaction with the black car attendant helps to displace issues of class division, offering instead the idea of equality between the classes based on a shared notion of whiteness.[12]

As Richard Abel documents in his account of the western's role in Americanizing cinema, the early film western was popular with urban immigrant audiences, the very people whom the eastern establishment demonized in its fictions, essays, and letters. According to Remington, solving the "problem" posed by immigrants was easy: "I've got some Winchesters and when the massacring begins. . . . I can get my share of 'em and what's more I will. Jews—Injuns—Chinamen—Italians—Huns—the rubbish of the earth I hate."[13] The cowboy's portrayal in literature, Wild West shows, theatrical dramas, paintings, mass-produced illustrations, and popular histories transformed him from a historically anonymous wage earner into a protomythical figure. The cowboy in early western films retains the potency of these incarnations, but his actions are played out on a greatly diminished stage. In this version the cowboy is neither a wage slave nor a mythical figure. Able to master the shocks of modernity, the early film cowboy (as a white male) successfully negotiates the divisions between labor and capital, urban and rural, work and leisure. Most significantly, the basis of his appeal is the appearance that the restrictions on his sovereignty are self-imposed rather than externally prescribed.

Though almost one quarter of all films produced in the United States during the 1910s were westerns, this figure includes Indian pictures. This type of film concentrated on Native American life and drama, often with no appreciable role for white characters. Furthermore, rival manufacturers produced different types of western stories. Early Selig westerns emphasized the authenticity and grandeur of their films' locations. Essanay promoted "Broncho Billy" Anderson as its main western attraction. Bison teamed up with the Miller Brothers' 101 Ranch Wild West show and formed Bison 101 and, relative to Essanay, produced western spectaculars. Bison 101 got dramatic mileage out of the livestock, props, and performers supplied by the Wild West show by concentrating on cavalry and Indian films. Biograph, particularly in the films directed by D. W. Griffith, emphasized high-quality production values. Only Bison 101 competed with Biograph in terms of visual spectacle, but the latter's productions are more visually and dramatically arresting.

These companies also produced a number of westerns that actively sought to address a female audience through the use of the "cowboy-girl," which strongly suggests, as Abel notes, "that young girls, even middle-class white girls, could be attracted to the genre." Further, the "surveys of children's viewing behavior, which proliferated in this period and concluded that boys, not girls, were the target audience for westerns, may be more representative of reformers' efforts to regulate leisure activities and channel children's desires according to conventional gender roles."[14] Moreover, as Eileen Bowser has noted, the film program during the 1910s offered a balanced bill of fare, where equally popular genres such as comedies and dramas played alongside the western.[15] An exhibitor who strung together an exclusive program of western dramas and still expected to please his audience would have been foolhardy.

Despite these points of differentiation, and there are many others, a particular narrative formula dominated the western of the period; it was not, as is commonly held, drawn from the dime novel, nor from Wister, Roosevelt, and Remington, but from the story types described by Robert Ohmann that first appeared in turn-of-the-century magazines addressed to the newly formed professional-managerial class. Set in the present, these stories are principally concerned with small acts of redemption: "Transgression of the law is the key, even when writers mine the West for humorous narrative and thus lower the moral stakes. . . . Stories of crime tend to gravitate toward the Western, as transgression opens up the possibility of reform and justification by a higher law."[16] Ohmann suggests that acts of transgression in the western are not "really about overriding the staple laws" but about defining "manliness." The plots that Ohmann describes are remarkably similar to those used in early film westerns, particularly the archetypal Broncho Billy scenario of the "good-bad man."

The film often does not reveal the criminal act that establishes the cowboy as a "bad man." In *Broncho Billy and the Sheriff's Kid* (Essanay, 1913) and the *Outlaw and the Child* (Essanay, 1911) the films begin with the "bad man" in jail, his crimes unreported. In *Sierra Jim's Reformation* (Majestic, 1914), *Broncho Billy's Squareness* (Essanay, 1913), *A Brother's Devotion* (Vitagraph, 1910), and *The Loafer's Mother* (Essanay, 1912), the transgression is an act of thievery motivated by the promise of immediate material gain. The transgressor has the chance of redemption by later performing an act of selflessness, often putting his own life at risk by saving a child or rescuing a woman in distress. However, these plots always swiftly punish sexual transgression, such as acts of seduction and particularly miscegenation.

Ohmann notes that transgressions are justified by "good works that benefit children, women, families, or lovers who want to start families. . . . Justice regularly demands that individuals humanize the law and so renew the social compact." The ideological work of these stories is to assure "readers whose life chances depend irrevocably on the urban, corporate order, that individual action and character still count."[17] However, the early film westerns are class conscious and therefore differ from the stories that Ohmann discusses. His stories efface class conflict, whereas the early film western suggests that such conflict is the greatest threat to the social contract. The films adapt the narrative formula observed in magazine fiction while continuing the tradition of social engagement established in the dime novels. They used the popular magazine formula because it could more ably conform to the temporal limitations of single-reel films (approximately ten minutes) than could the meandering dime novel narratives. But beyond this obvious pragmatism, the recurring motif of redemption also suggests the possibility of a new start in life—that where you begin does not necessarily determine where you end.

With the U.S. film industry's shift in production from single-reel films to multireel features in the early to mid-1910s, "Broncho Billy" Anderson's cowboy career ended. Two actors then dominated western filmmaking during the remainder of the silent period, or at least they dominate the histories of western films: Tom Mix and William S. Hart. But what of the western movie itself? To what point had it evolved by the late 1920s, when the introduction of sound in Hollywood made the singing cowboy a technical possibility? It is easy to assume that because the singing cowboy came along, the movies had developed in such a way that his appearance was a natural outcome of what had gone before. This is indeed the way conventional film history tells it. Accepted histories of the genre see Hart and Mix as representing diverse, even opposed, tendencies in the western: on the one hand, a genre rooted in the harsh realities of life in the West—austere moral tales of sturdy and stoic heroes defending the weak in a lawless land—and on the other hand, sensational stories of violent action replete with gunfights and chases on horseback and shot through with romance and humor.

According to these accounts, William S. Hart is descended from the archetype first encountered in Owen Wister's 1902 novel, *The Virginian* (Hart had played in a stage version), and is the forebear of all those stars who have lent weight and gravitas to the western, a tradition that encompasses John Wayne, Randolph Scott, and Clint Eastwood. Tom Mix, on the other hand, with his repertoire of stunts, his liking for pranks, his innocent high spirits, leads in a different direction entirely. His origins are not on the Victorian stage but in the culturally disreputable arenas of the Wild West show and the circus, and Mix's lack of high seriousness, coupled with his liking for flamboyant costume, reveals him as the antecedent of a different kind of western hero, one whose status places him at the bottom of a genre that in itself has always struggled for cultural standing. Mix can then be seen as the forerunner of the singing cowboys of the 1930s, a phenomenon immensely popular in its day and largely neglected since by all serious students of the western.

At least, that is the received view. In practice things are not so clearcut. Hart and Mix did have very different starts to their film careers, beginnings that would influence their apparently distinct cowboy masquerades. Hart had been a professional stage actor for twenty years before he began making films in 1914. Roles in *The Squaw Man* and *The Virginian* allowed Hart to play out his cowboy fantasies on stage, and the recognition that he received following these Broadway shows eventually brought him to the attention of Thomas Ince and the New York Motion Picture Company. Though born in the West, Hart spent most of his professional life before his move to Hollywood in the East.

Tom Mix can be seen on the left in this production still from *Riders of the Purple Sage* (1925). Numerous publicity images of silent and sound series western stars were used in which the film production process was staged, as it is here.

Writing to Charlie Russell, the cowboy artist, whom he first met in 1902, Hart called forth his romanticized notion of western life: "The range with a boundless view of the naked plains—would be the place of all places on earth for me and if ever in later years it is my fortune to strike a lucky streak and make my little pile it will be in that west I love so well that I will pitch my tent and end my days." But like Russell, Hart understood this West as belonging to the past: "When I look at these mountains and plains out here and then at your pictures which speak as no language can of a whole race that is forever gone—I feel a great deal."[18] Hart's maudlin and sentimental view of the West—a mawkish melancholia—carried over into many of his films. Despite those critics who find in Hart's western morality tales an authentic representation of western life, his films no more correspond to the "real" than do the "frivolous" western films of Tom Mix.[19]

Appropriately, Tom Mix's prefilm biography is wrapped in mystery and myth: was he a Spanish-American War hero, a mercenary in the Boer War, a combatant in the Philippine insurrection, a Texas Ranger? Not likely—but he was, as the western film historian Buck Rainey has written, a "showman *nonpareil*."[20] Between 1905 and 1912 Mix appeared in a number of Wild West shows, including the 101 Ranch Show. He made his first appearance in films in 1909 as a featured rider in *Ranch Life in the Great South West* (Selig). Shot at some distance from the action, the film shows various riders performing tricks familiar to Wild West show audiences. Mix adapted for the movies the flamboyant persona and riding tricks that he had developed in those shows.

Hart's background, austere costumes, and stoic physiognomy proclaimed him an "actor." Mix's background, daring stunts, roping skills, elaborate costumes, and happy visage proclaimed him a "performer." The distinction is important because film historians have classified Hart's films according to their appeal for adults, whereas Mix is said to have appealed to children. Neither representation is true. Both Hart and Mix earned phenomenal salaries, and the films they produced at the height of their careers were highly profitable.[21] Hart and Mix may have appealed to different sensibilities, but their appeal crossed generation and gender (though probably not class) lines—the western remained a staple working-class preference. Hart would even make a mildly prolabor film, *The Whistle* (Famous Players–Lasky, 1921), which exposed unsafe factory practices and working conditions.

The established divisions between Mix and Hart are testament to a critical connivance and convenience that seek to construct an orderly

William S. Hart in a typically stern pose in this publicity still from *Tollgate* (1920).

map of development within the history of western films. This "family tree" describes an early bifurcation from the root and trunk that grew out of *The Virginian*. Hart's "authentic" West forms the main branch, with the subsequent branches forming the "adult" A-feature westerns that reach "maturity" in the late 1930s. Mix's "flamboyant" West forms a weaker branch that will eventually hold the B westerns and the singing cowboys. But this historical teleology—the end is foretold in the beginning—is too simplistic to account for the complexity of the figure of the film cowboy, which exceeds such a reductive bifurcation.

Mix, for example, could be every bit as austere as Hart. After making a large number of one- and two-reel films for Selig, Mix went to work for William Fox. Fox's resources assured that Mix received ample exposure. In early film adaptations of B. M. Bower's stories, as well as in scripts by other female writers such as Emma Bell, Mabel Heikes Justice, and Hettie Gray Baker, Mix established the role of the "flirt-and-run" cowboy (Buck Rainey's description). Mix continued with this characterization at Fox, but he also crossed over into Hart's territory in film adaptations of Max Brand's early novels, *The Untamed* (Fox, 1920), *The Night Horsemen* (Fox, 1921), and *Trailin'* (Fox, 1921). These films, and others like them, such as the Zane Grey adaptations *Riders of the Purple Sage* (Fox, 1925), *Rainbow Trail* (Fox, 1925), and *The Last of the Duanes* (Fox, 1924), matched the "realism" of Hart's Old West. In *Riders of the Purple Sage* Mix's early characterization epitomizes the coldhearted gunfighter. He kills without remorse, as Hart had done in films such as *Hell's Hinges* (Triangle, 1916). And while *Sage* offers some spectacular stunts and riding sequences, Mix does not embrace his horse at the end in preference to the heroine. Apart from removing all references to Mormons, the film remains faithful to its source material.

Hart, on the other hand, could not or would not cross over into the more lighthearted material at which Mix excelled. This inflexibility in his choice of roles, alongside his lack of youthful vigor, may help explain his fall from grace as the nation's leading box-office cowboy and Mix's subsequent rise to preeminence. Hart's last film, *Tumbleweeds* (William S. Hart Co./UA, 1925), was an attempt to exploit the cycle of western epics that had begun so promisingly with *The Covered Wagon* (Paramount, 1923) and continued with *The Iron Horse* (Fox, 1924). However, despite the terrific closing spectacle of the race for land, this story of the opening for settlement of the Cherokee Strip in Oklahoma did not revitalize Hart's career, nor did it add much novelty to the historical representation of the "winning of the West," which had been shown with such grandiose effect in earlier epics.

The problem is that historians have tended to equate Hart's solemnity with seriousness and Mix's lightness of heart with childishness. Discussing what he considers to be the waning appeal of westerns between 1915 and 1928, Richard Koszarski writes: "The change in public taste was predictable, because Westerns had moved from the serious plateau of the early DeMille pictures to a genre clearly intended for children. The form ultimately became so degraded that Westerns were the only genre segregated from the balance of a studio's product line (as in '. . . and eight Westerns')."[22] Considered from the perspective of a middle-class aesthetic, the western appears childish and naive, offering simple, innocent pleasures. Koszarski measures the silent western's degradation against DeMille's adaptations of *The Squaw Man* (Lasky Feature Play Co., 1914) and *The Virginian* (Paramount, 1914), stories that represent an embourgeoisement of the western, imparting due weight and seriousness to the genre. Despite Koszarski's comments, and

Richard Slotkin's claim that *The Virginian* is the paradigm of western films, westerns produced after DeMille's flirtation with the genre (or even before) are not impoverished, low, or degraded versions.

The problem is in applying inappropriate criteria. Westerns clearly fall far short of the mark when measured against bourgeois notions of taste, where the demand is for narratives and characters that conform to prevailing discourses of realism. But Jack Hoxie, Hoot Gibson, and Ken Maynard, for example, are best viewed not as "actors" but as "performers." Their films promote action and spectacle, not narrative coherence. The intended audience of the series western values the exhibition of performance (which disrupts an "invisible" unfolding of narrative events linked through cause and effect). Hollywood clearly recognized that these westerns had a distinct audience, which is why production was "segregated," not because it was "degraded." The spectacle of stunts, trick riding, buffoonery, fistfights, and so forth created a pleasurable stalling of the inevitable plot trajectory. These sequences upset an established order of things. This is linked to characterizations that operate upon transparency of disguise and false identities. Such overt distrust of appearances and fixed notions of a social contract contest rather than affirm stabilized notions of character and status displayed in bourgeois fictions.

To view westerns from a mind-set predicated on bourgeois notions of good taste constitutes a misreading. Koszarski notes that Jack Hoxie's *The Western Whirlwind* (Universal, 1927) was made for $15,935.44 and grossed five times that amount. In 1926 Tom Mix was earning $15,000 *per week*.[23] The pocket money of children cannot, alone, account for the profits from his films (as well as those of other western stars). The suggestion that westerns were only suitable for, and were predominantly consumed by, children ignores the complex cultural heritage and performance traditions upon which the genre drew and that lie outside bourgeois canons of cultural value.

The promotional gambits that the studio used to exploit Ken Maynard's westerns reveal the breadth of attractions designed to appeal to a diverse audience, in particular adult patrons. After Maynard's performance in several supporting roles at Fox Studios, the independent studio Davis Distributing put him under contract in 1925 to star in eight features. Boosting his reputation as a rodeo and circus trick rider, the company centered its promotion on the promise of thrilling riding stunts. Publicity for *Fighting Courage*, the second of five films that Maynard would complete for the company, described it as a "West-

ern stunt film drama—it's just full of action punch thrills and love."
The film's press book opens with two "personal messages": the company's president confers on Maynard the accolade of being a "real
cowboy actor" who has earned his spurs working for some of the great
circuses, including the Ringling Brothers and Barnum and Bailey Circus. The second is from Maynard, who gives his "personal pledge" that
he will never "under any circumstances deceive" his fans by permitting
anyone else to "risk his life in my behalf"—all stunts will be performed
by one man "and that man will be KEN MAYNARD."[24] In the section
called "Stories That Will Go Over," which provides ready-for-print news
stories about the film and its actors for the exhibitor to use in plug-
ging the film in the local press, the film's stunt work remains in the
fore but sits alongside the film's other offered attractions.

The film also offers comedy, in the guise of Sambo, played by James
Berry, a seven-year-old "little colored boy," who draws from a "broad
experience to furnish many laugh-provoking scenes." This "news" item
is headlined "PICANINNY MAKES GOOD." The "stories" also tout the
film's spectacular landscapes: "Background and scenic effects are important to all pictures [and] the Davis Distribution Division has spared
neither time nor expense in securing the most beautiful and appropri-
ate settings." Maynard's horse, Tarzan, receives space alongside a number of the film's character actors, but the press book reserves far and
away the greatest ballyhoo for the pitch to both male and female film
goers: the film's novelty of six New York chorus girls stranded out West.
The film bills the women as "The Hollywood Beauty Sextette." Clearly
designed as a titillating come-on to male viewers, the publicity nevertheless stresses the potential for gaining female interest through items about
how the Sextette members keep their figures trim (dancing and a "rig-
orous course of physical training") and about other beauty enhance-
ments, such as plastic surgery. The publicity reports that one starlet until
recently had "possessed a proboscis that was anything but pleasing."

Another ploy to attract female interest was placing an advertisement
in the press in the form of a letter headlined "GIRLS! KEN MAY-
NARD'S COMING TO TOWN—YOU MUST SEE THIS PULSATING
PICTURE"—"Dear Madam," begins the "letter," and it ends by stressing the promise of "thrills" and "love-making." The copy uses the contemporary advertising penchant for pseudo-Freudian psychoanalysis
in order to exploit sublimated female desire—a pulsating Ken. Illustrated advertising promoted a dual appeal to male and female viewers. In a pair of linked advertisements one is principally addressed to

A "pulsating" Ken Maynard.

female punters: "JAZZ MAD! How could the poor kid tell she was clop-ing with the jazziest sheik in town!" The one addressed to men reads: "Kingsley at last had come across The Mystery Bandit who was at the root of all his trouble. He was to get even at last!" The address may be gender specific, but the advertisements are also designed to appeal to both genders. In the advertisement addressed to men the threat of violent action sits alongside an illustration that also highlights romantic intrigue, and a reversal of the same ploy pitched the film to women.

This film's press book makes no direct appeal to children. In all likelihood the studio took this audience for granted. The *Exhibitors Trade Review* recommended that managers "run special matinees for the juveniles," but it had earlier highlighted the film's adult attractions: "Ken Maynard, who plays the lead, is a good looking chap who will appeal to both men and women. He has a pleasant smile, and a ready pair of hands. Truly, a combination devoutly to be wished."[25]

Following his series of films for Davis, Maynard landed a contract with First National. The press book for *The Overland Stage* (1927) continued to promote the star both as an extraordinary stunt rider and a cowboy with sex appeal: "Go to the Palace Tonight and Get All Pepped Up over Ken Maynard's New Picture—He is just about the warmest lover the screen offers and the most daring 'daredevil.'" "Hell bent for Romance! Give him a Girl and a Gun!" "At-a-boy, Ken! He sure can Love . . . he sure can Ride!" Ken, though, is "essentially what is known as a 'man's man,' although recent fan mail received at First National Studios indicate that women admirers are increasing since the release of *Senor Daredevil*." The press books that accompanied this season's series of films developed the idea of the "cowboy star with sex appeal": "Ken's fan mail from flappers would rival any amount of letters received by a star of the 'sheik' type"—a man's man, indeed.[26] The lead item in the press book for *The Overland Stage* details just exactly what Ken likes in a woman, and it is worth quoting at length:

> "I like a thoroughbred. . . . A woman who shows her good breeding in her walk, her manner, her attitude toward life and her sportsmanship. Beauty in a woman is a matter of fineness, of mettle and of spirit!"
>
> Thoroughbreds, Maynard contends, are not confined to any particular class, or nationality, and are born, not made.
>
> "The most exquisite woman I ever saw in my life was sitting on a boxcar top near a railroad station in a little desert town eating a ham sandwich. She had grace, beauty and charm, that even her poor clothes could not hide."
>
> He has no objection to women using powder, lipstick or rouge, but hopes the fashion for men to do likewise will never come about.

The class address is explicit—you do not have to be rich to be attractive. So too is the validation of modern femininity expressed through the consumption of cosmetics. The appeal to female viewers to identify with the modern heroine in Maynard's and other series westerns would continue into the 1930s. The development of Maynard's female fan base was carried out not only in the publicity that surrounded the films but also in the roles that he played, notably in a series of south-of-the-border westerns in which he was dressed in tight-fitting Mexican costumes. Despite the denial that Maynard shared any similarities with the feminized Latin lovers of the screen ("sheiks" such as Valentino), exotic character types and locations allowed for greater play with romantic situations—though Maynard would usually only be masquerading as a Mexican.

Furthermore, female scriptwriters played a major role. Marion Jackson wrote nearly all of Maynard's First National pictures, while other female writers (such as Adele Buffington and Sylvia Seid) worked on some films in which Jackson did not participate. Later, Betty Burbridge, who would have a key role in writing many of Autry's films, was employed to supply the story on a number of Maynard's early talkies.

The pitch made in the press book for Maynard's *The Land Beyond the Law* (First National, 1927) best sums up the diverse audience appeal of the 1920s series western: "If you like action, and at the same time ask that you be given nothing impossible to believe; if you like romance and dislike sentimentality with it, if you like adventure and don't want fairytales as a substitute—don't fail to see *The Land Beyond the Law*." The film promises romance and adventure, and, as another film's press book suggests, it has attractions enough for all tastes: "Take the kiddies, mother, sister, sweetheart, grandpa—or If you're economizing just go yourself—but don't miss this red-blooded picture."[27]

The series western sought to be inclusive in its cross-generation and -gender address, to exclude no one. Yet in its promotion of the performance of spectacle rather than narrative causality and psychological realism, it displayed a class consciousness that marginalized its appeal to a middle-class audience. Nevertheless, marked out in terms of performance traditions, it is possible to recognize the figure of the movie cowboy not as a degraded or debased character but as culturally complex, historically rooted, and multidimensional. This is particularly so in his fabrication as the performer and subject of popular song.

From at least *Fighting Courage* to the end of Ken Maynard's contract with First National in 1929, the promotional department consistently suggested that theater owners feature a prologue of live entertainment by a group of musicians dressed in cowboy duds and singing cowboy songs: "Around a camp fire sit four cowboys and as the curtain rises they begin their first number. Of course the stage is dark, the only illumination coming from the campfire. With the conclusion of the first song turn on the stage lights. . . . At the conclusion of the last number sung by the cowboys flash out all of the lights for a few seconds and when the house is again illuminated the quartette will appear in evening clothes which they wear under their cowboy outfits. This will take the audience by surprise."[28] Slipping in and out of cowboy costumes became a major habit for southern musicians who were trying to break into the newly emerging radio and recording industries. By the mid-1930s their domination of the series western would revolutionize the form, along with the public's conception of cowboy songs.

THREE

Monodies for the Cowpuncher:
Cowboy Songs and Singers

In *The Seven Lively Arts* (1924) Gilbert Seldes offers an opinion then unique among American intelligentsia—a Keystone Kops slapstick comedy or a Krazy Kat cartoon had as much merit as was usually associated with "Art." He argues of popular music:

> The popular song takes its place between the folk song and the art song. Of these the folk song hardly exists in America to-day: "Casey Jones" and "Frankie and Johnny" are examples of what we possess and one doesn't often hear them sung along country roads or by brown armed men at the rudder in ships that go down to the sea. The songs of the Kentucky mountains (English in provenance) and the old cowboy songs are both the object of antiquarian interest—they aren't as alive as the universal "Hail, Hail, the Gang's All Here" or "We Won't Go Home 'til Morning."[1]

By collapsing the positive values thought to be held within the antonyms *folk* and *art,* Seldes sought to find the "vitality" authenticated

46

in American folk song and the "intellectual" creativity of the legitimate arts also present in the popular. As a New York critic writing in the mid-1920s, his comprehension of cowboy songs as belonging to the past and as having only "antiquarian interest" is understandable. The common conception of a dichotomy between an authentic and a commercial cowboy musical idiom began to take form in the late 1920s and was fully established by the mid-1930s when Gene Autry made his first film appearances. Seldes was writing at a time when cowboy songs, through published collections, had obtained a profile as an authentic folk form but had yet to be fully exploited by the relatively new media of radio, phonograph recordings, and, after 1927 with synchronized sound, by the movies.

As authentic American folk song, cowboy songs first gained a degree of national recognition with the publication of John A. Lomax's *Cowboy Songs and Other Frontier Ballads* (1910). Though far from being a publishing sensation, the collection would act as *the* primer for all subsequent anthologies of cowboy songs and was responsible for the broad dissemination of songs that now constitute a common recognition of the form: "Jesse James," "The Old Chisholm Trail," "Whoopie Ti Yi Yo, Git Along, Little Dogies," and "Home on the Range." This was the start of Lomax's career as a "ballad hunter," placing him as the foremost U.S. authority on folk song in the first half of the twentieth century.

Raised on a small Texas farm, Lomax was a tireless "self-improver" who, after taking leave of absence from his post teaching English at the Agricultural and Mechanical College of Texas, enrolled at Harvard in 1904 to undertake postgraduate courses. Under the tutelage of Barrett Wendell and George Lyman Kittredge (a founding member of the American Folklore Society), Lomax began to collect songs. Kittredge was an enthusiastic reader and teacher of Francis James Child's collection *The English and Scottish Popular Ballads* (1882–96), an original work in the academic establishment of an "essential" British folk culture. Using Child's work as their model, Wendell and Kittredge sought to confirm a similar cultural significance for American folk art. Lomax's efforts in documenting the West's musical culture would form an important part of this project.

Though Lomax's work on cowboy songs had its immediate origins within the rarefied air of the academy, the end result was removed from it. "Frankly," he wrote, "the volume is meant to be popular."[2] Rather than a scrupulous piece of field research, Lomax's collection features songs gathered through requests to newspaper readers and, despite his claim to the contrary, from previously published collections. He culled nineteen from N. Howard (Jack) Thorp's privately published book, *Songs of the Cowboys* (1908).[3] Regardless of its dubious provenance, Lomax's book was, as his biographer Nolan Porterfield claims, "if not in fact, then certainly in substance and in effect—simply the first important collection of American folk song."[4]

Porterfield has identified an early essay by Lomax, "The Minstrelsy of the Mexican Border," which appeared without a byline in the January 1898 issue of the *University of Texas Magazine*. The title, as Porterfield notes, owes a debt to Sir Walter Scott's *Minstrelsy of the Scottish Border*. Lomax analyses several cowboy songs that would appear in his 1910 collection and closes with a eulogy to a vanishing West: "Better things, it may be, are coming in to take the place of the cowboys, but to these as the years go by, will be added a glamour that the things that have driven them into the west and down to death can never hold. No furrowed field can ever make a man forget the prairies and the magic of their call when Spring is breaking, no harvest gathering can ever equal the rough assemblage of the round-up, and no man in all the world can ever take the vacant place of 'the last cavalier.'"[5] By invoking the image of the cowboy as "the last cavalier," Lomax demonstrates his familiarity with Owen Wister's essay "The Evolution of the Cow-Puncher," published only eighteen months earlier, in 1895. Frederic Remington illustrated Wister's essay, and the picture "The Last Cavalier" graphically traces the cowboy's evolution from medieval knights. Moreover, both the elegiac tones of Lomax's essay and his title's allusion to Scott support this conjecture of influence. In "Evolution" Wister considers the cowboy a suitably romantic figure who yet lacks an author: "If his raids, his triumphs, and his reverses have inspired no minstrel to sing of him who rode by the Pecos River and the hills of San Andreas, it is not so much the Rob Roy as the Walter Scott who is lacking."[6]

After the publication of *The Virginian* Wister, with some justification, saw himself as the American Scott, just as Lomax with *Cowboy Songs* was the recording angel of the "minstrels" who sang of the cowpuncher's feats. That Lomax shared a sensibility with Theodore Roosevelt, Wister, and Remington in his romanticization of the West is evident in Lomax's dedication of the book to Roosevelt and in his having Roosevelt write an endorsement—a facsimile of which was published in the first and subsequent editions: "There is something very curious in the reproduction here on this continent of essentially the conditions of ballad growth which obtained in medieval England, including, by the way, sympathy for the outlaw Jesse James taking the place of Robin Hood."

More curious was that Lomax reproduced in a subsequent edition a cowboy song written by Owen Wister, "Ten Thousand Cattle Straying" [1904] (written to be sung by Trampas in the stage adaptation of *The Virginian*). Lomax passed it off as a genuine example of the cowboy's musical heritage. The process involved in this translation of a commercially composed song into a folk song is instructive and reveals the difficulty that folk song collectors have subsequently had in untangling the authentic from the commercial. In fact, as a number of folk song detectives have shown, little in the canon of American folk is not "despoiled" by the commercial. In *Git Along Little Dogies: Songs and Songmakers of the American West*, John I. White reveals the tangled history of a number of cowboy songs, the most telling of which is the story of "Home on the Range."[7] Lomax claimed to have obtained the song from a black saloon keeper in San Antonio two years before the publication of his book in 1910. Between 1925 and 1934 White collected a dozen sheet music editions of the song by various publishers, with only one credited to Lomax. As a song considered in the public domain, it was fair game for any enterprising publisher who sought to profit from the song's increasing popularity, helped no end by radio and record performances. However, the publishing bonanza came to an abrupt halt in 1934 when William and Mary Goodwin filed suit in federal court in New York; they claimed that "Home on the Range" was a version of their song "An Arizona Home," copyrighted in 1905. They named twenty-nine copyright infringers and sought $500,000 in compensation. Notified earlier that the Goodwins intended to file suit, the defendants had hired a lawyer to track down earlier versions of the song and prove the song belonged in the public domain. Before the formal filing of the Goodwin claim, the lawyer for the defendants authenticated a version written in 1885 through a 1914 newspaper clipping but was unable to trace the original lyrics that the article claimed had first appeared in 1873. Nevertheless, the lawyer had amassed enough evidence to compel the Goodwins to drop their litigation. In 1945 a researcher uncovered a version of the song published in an 1876 edition of a Kansas newspaper, and this appeared to be the end of the trail. However, in one of the last collections of folk songs that he published before his death in 1947, Lomax argues the song had no "ultimate origin."[8]

The difficulty that folk song collectors encountered in their search for "unadulterated" examples of cowboy songs was that the cowboy had become inseparable from the image created by mass popular culture. Even if the claimed author of a particular song was a cowboy, White's histories inevitably led back to the song's first *publication*. Moreover, as with Wister's "Ten Thousand Cattle Straying," the songs would often be produced to accompany western dramas and fiction. "The Cowboy's Sweet By and By," a song that appears in many anthologies of cowboy songs, is illustrative. First published in an 1895 issue of *Cosmopolitan Magazine,* it was sung by the central character in a short story written by Will Croft Barnes. In 1925 Barnes recounted how he first heard the song while riding the range in northern Arizona. He wrote down the song, sung to the tune of "My Bonnie Lies over the Ocean," with the "idea of using it as a motif for a cowboy story."[9] After Barnes published the story, another writer of short western fiction appropriated the song without giving credit. Then, in 1897, it appeared (again without credit) in the trade journal *Field and Farm.* Thorp printed yet another version in his 1908 collection, while a magazine article on cowboy songs, also published in 1908, added new verses and finally gave Barnes credit. A version in Mary M. North's novel *A Prairie-Schooner: A Romance of the Plains of Kansas* (1902) used a different title, but the tune is the same. However, in keeping with the sentimental mode of the story, North's setting is not the range but a domestic context: "It became the custom for the two friends to meet at the home of Eva, as soon as the shadows of evening began to fall, and then there was music until the hour of parting. Mrs. Deming had a fine alto voice. Eva sang soprano, and accompanied herself on guitar, while Horace sang tenor, and Herbert added his deep bass tones. A favorite song and one that could be heard any evening was the cowboy's song, 'The Lost Trail,' sung to the tune of 'My Bonnie Lies Over the Ocean.'"[10] Regardless of whether working cowboys actually sang the tune, reworked and rewritten, its appropriation had commercial aims in mind—a palimpsest, with the original (if indeed such a thing ever existed) long since obscured.

In his provocative critical evaluation of U.S. folklorists, Gene Bluestein notes that any attempt to establish an American folk tradition conceptualized along lines similar to those that existed in Britain and Europe is doomed to failure: "Very little of what developed in American folklore took place without the influence of strong popular and commercial sources. . . . In American tradition, many different forms of folk style exist, all 'contaminated' by levels of culture beyond the pale of what scholars have defined as authentically traditional."[11]

Cowboy songs exemplify this process of the combination of folk and commerce. "The Cowboy's By and By" borrowed its tune from an old British ballad, and other equally famous songs such as "The Streets of Laredo" were similarly based on old British airs. While this might suggest the vitality of the folk process of adaptation and reinvention, cowboy songs could as easily be reworked blackface minstrel tunes first popularized on urban stages in the North. Indeed, turn-of-the-century western fiction is just as likely to give its cowboy protagonists a minstrel air to sing on the range as it is to provide a now more familiar western refrain.

In *The Log of a Cowboy* (1903) Andy Adams writes: "There is such a thing as cowboy music. It is a hybrid between the weirdness of an Indian cry and the croon of the black mammy. It expresses the open, the prairies, the immutable desert."[10] Adams includes snatches of "Git Along, Little Dogies" in his history of the cattle trail, but he also has his cowboys singing minstrel tunes:

> Two little niggers upstairs in bed,
> One turned ober to de oder an' said
> "How 'bout dat shortnin' bread,
> How 'bout dat shortnin' bread?"[13]

Similarly, Wister's eponymous hero in *The Virginian* sings minstrel songs:

> "Yes, he'll be a missionary," said the Virginian, conclusively; and he took
> to singing, or rather to whining, with his head tilted at an absurd angle upward at the sky:
>
> > "Dar is a big Car'lina nigger,
> > About de size of dis chile or p'raps a little bigger,
> > By de name of Jim Crow.
> > Dat what de white folks call him."[14]

As do Emerson Hough's cowboys in his 1897 history: "'Oh, then, Susannah, don't yer cry fer me!' sings another voice, as the owner of it, wrapped in his yellow slicker, gets into his saddle and turns towards the herd."[15] Hough also gives one of the earliest reports of cowboys singing to quiet the herd at night.[16]

The minstrel tunes in these stories signify the protagonists' déclassé status. In some of B. M. Bower's tales she draws upon a more modern manifestation of blackface minstrelsy, the "coon song": "'I do wish—'

The Little Doctor checked herself abruptly, and hummed a bit of a coon song." According to the historian of popular American music Charles Hamm, "coon songs" were the fifth and last stage in the development of the minstrel song. The first stage was the antebellum "nigger song" such as "Old Dan Tucker" and "Jim Crow." The plantation song of which Stephen Foster is the prime exponent followed this. The third stage was the postwar song style exemplified by the nostalgic sentiments of "Carry Me Back to Old Virginny" and "The Old Home Ain't What It Used to Be." The fourth stage, the minstrel-spiritual, was popularized by the Fisk Jubilee Singers in the 1870s and speedily appropriated by white performers. The "coon song" was in some respects a return to the "nigger song." Both eschewed nostalgia and any notion of spiritual uplift. Yet the "coon song" plumbed depths of racial caricature unseen before or since in American popular culture. The fad for "coon songs" lasted almost forty years, between 1880 and 1920, and became synonymous with a number of vaudeville's greatest stars. Among those who bore the epithet "coon shouter" were Sophie Tucker, May Irwin, Norah Bayes, Dolly Connolly, Billy Murray, Bert Williams (the first African-American Broadway star), and Al Jolson. For the most part the songs were delivered as comedies, because without the distancing effect of humor the listener was confronted with the frightening image of the African American as vicious and bestial. The "coon song" has no saving graces, and many historians of popular song prefer to concentrate their studies of the era on the parallel development of ragtime, which allows them to make a much less problematic transition to discussions of the development of jazz.[17]

The musical distraction of the "coon song" in Bower's story tacitly reveals the cultural bond between the eastern-educated doctor and the working cowboys. Earlier, the Flying U Ranch pals had been looking forward to a dance with the musical entertainment provided by a "coon band."[18] This is not to say that the happy family of the Flying U Ranch does not have more traditional cowboy musical divertissements. But as Bower acknowledges, these had already become so commercialized that she refers to the overstylized Stetsons worn by vacationing easterners as "cowboy hats of the musical comedy brand."[19] With cowboy music little lies between the commercial and the authentic.

Cowboy songs first began to appear on phonograph records in the mid- to late 1920s. The context in which they appeared would help confirm a sense of their authenticity, particularly when compared to later Tin Pan Alley, Broadway, and Hollywood compositions. With the arrival of radio, record sales to the urban middle classes—the principal consumers—dropped rapidly. In search of new customers phonograph companies sought to exploit the underdeveloped rural and race markets. With this end in mind companies used local rural representatives to seek out potential recording talent. One of the first field recording sessions that Ralph Peer conducted for the Okeh label secured the talents of Fiddlin' John Carson. Born in 1868, Carson had been performing regularly for years on a semiprofessional basis in and around Atlanta. Through appearances on local radio that began in 1922, the local Okeh representative knew that Carson had a significantly large number of listeners and recommended him to Peer as a potential recording artist. Carson promoted his first release through live performances and radio appearances. The first and subsequent pressing sold rapidly, and Carson was brought to New York in November 1923 to record about a dozen sides. For Peer the success of these sessions was proof that a large enough market existed for the company to work out a more systematic exploitation of rural talent for a rural market.[20]

Carson drew upon a broad spectrum of musical styles: square dance tunes, minstrel numbers, old ballads, nineteenth-century Tin Pan Alley tunes, and cowboy songs, material that would form the foundation of a new musical genre paradoxically called "old time." Indeed, many songs and styles were "old-fashioned" but only in the context of other popular song forms that urban performers then were producing. In time, as sales of old-time records boomed, the companies would need to create new old-time music. "By 1927," writes Richard Peterson, "Ralph Peer had come to see traditional music as a renewable resource, and he developed a system of production that committed creative singer-songwriters to the quest for new old-sounding songs."[21] The motivation for this process, which Peterson calls "fabricating authenticity," was commercial, and entrepreneurs like Ralph Peer set up their own highly lucrative publishing companies to exploit this "new" music. "By ferreting out musicians who, in the history of culture, belonged to the past," writes the music historian Robert Cantwell, "Peer exploited the *first principle* of recording technology, which is that it divides the sound from that which has produced the sound: the recorded performance itself is *always* in the past. . . . Expanding that gap until it became historical in scope, Peer sought to *bring back the past acoustically*. This was *cosmic* ventriloquism, catching a voice from the past. 'These rollicking melodies,' the Okeh catalog promises, 'will quicken the memory of the tunes of yesterday.'"[22]

Nostalgia played a large part in the eager consumption of these records, but Peterson quotes a contemporary editorial in a phonograph trade journal that says it was not the whole story: "The fact that the public or a fair portion of it has decided on a funeral dirge type of offering should not be taken as an atavistic tendency. It is rather a desire for something different."[23] Specifically, the writer hoped the craze for "hill-billy" songs marked the "passing of jazz." It did not, but old-time music suggested a continued taste for songs, in Seldes's phrase, "to be sung" as opposed to "songs to be played"; jazz exemplified the latter.[24]

The growing popularity of old-time music therefore must be set against its competition, jazz, which emerged at the same time. In this sense the publication of a number of histories and collections of nineteenth- and turn-of-the-century songs are counterreactions to the urban sounds of jazz that invoked the anxieties of modernity. The foremost exponent of this trend was the musicologist and newspaper columnist Sigmund Spaeth, who enjoyed considerable success with his collections *Read 'Em and Weep: The Songs You Forgot to Remember* (1926) and *Weep Some More, My Lady* (1927).[25] These erudite and popular volumes were joined by other titles, such as John Tasker Howard's *Our American Music* (1929); Frank Shay's *My Pious Friends and Drunken Companions* (1927) and *More Pious Friends and Drunken Companions* (1928); and James J. Geller's *Famous Songs and their Stories* (1931), which concludes with a chapter called "Before Jazz."[26] The fad for jazz became the line that divided an "old" from a "new" American music, as in Helen L. Kaufmann's popular history, *From Jehovah to Jazz: Music in America from Psalmody to the Present Day* (1937).[27] Alongside these avowedly nostalgic trips down a musical memory lane, publishers brought out a flurry of histories and collections of American folk song, including Guy B. Johnson's *John Henry: Tracking Down a Negro Legend* (1929), and Newman I. White's *American Negro Folk-Songs* (1928).[28] Lomax published a second volume of cowboy songs in 1919 and with his son, Alan, published *American Folk Songs and Ballads* (1934).[29] But the poet Carl Sandburg published the most popular and a vastly influential collection in 1927; *The American Songbag* quite simply defined the popular conception of American folk song.[30]

These histories and folk and pop collections share a significant number of songs, and more duplications occur in the material recorded by old-time musicians. Unlike jazz (which Spaeth would neatly define as the "distortion of the conventions of popular music"), these songs take on the appearance of a lost world, the door to which opens out upon a bittersweet nostalgic vista.[31] Discussing Bill Monroe's compositions, which exude tradition—he would, after all, become the inventor of bluegrass—Robert Cantwell writes:

> It is amusing, perhaps, that Bill can claim to have written an old fiddle tune; but in the paradox is an insight into traditional music, which is simply that on account of its thoroughgoing conventionality its location in time, which cannot be reliably fixed on the basis of internal evidence, has no effect upon its meaning: we might as well attempt to write a history of cloud formations. For Monroe, 'old' is simply a metaphor for the quality of mystery, majesty, or simplicity no strictly original work—if there is such a thing—can achieve.[32]

Cantwell says that Monroe's compositions (the most famous of which was "Blue Moon of Kentucky") use devices similar to those of romantic poets: "a narrative frame, an archaic language, a wild or picturesque setting, mysterious or magical events, and a careful exclusion of particularizing or historicizing detail in favor of the general and universal."[33] Cantwell suggests that this is a world similar to that of traditional English ballads and Irish reels and, by extension, of the old-time music recorded in the mid- to late 1920s. From the latter Monroe learned and developed the style now known as bluegrass. In the context of old-time music, the West becomes a part of this archaic universe: familiar names, events, and places help locate the songs in a recognizable historical (and firmly American) past, but the performances obscure their particularity, shrouding it in mystery—suggesting a lost world peopled by phantoms.

No recording illustrates this more effectively than the two sides that Dick Devall cut in 1929: "Tom Sherman's Barroom" and "Out on the Lone Star Cow Trail."[34] He renders both a cappella, and his rough untutored phrasing lends a haunting ambience to the familiar "Tom Sherman's Barroom" (a.k.a. "Streets of Laredo" and "Cowboy's Lament"). The music appears lost in the ether, the limits of the recording device shutting the voice off from its immediate surroundings and setting it adrift in isolation. The performance summons up the narrator, emerging perhaps from the pool room of Sherman's bar; with cue in hand he joins the growing crowd that, from afar, looks upon a dying cowboy—all wrapped in white linen and waiting to die, the scene at once both mundane and spectral. The song has been heard many times, yet the image of the dying cowboy, too soon entombed in his

white shroud, draws the listener back. As the dying cowboy asks the
narrator to tell his mother of the fate that befell him, he is in effect
offering a mantra common to many cowboy songs. For every tale of
derring-do out on the range, a dozen are laments for fallen comrades:

> In a far-off western country where friends are few and dear
> Stands a humble little headstone 'neath a sky that's always clear.
> And the rancher's little daughter now often comes to pray
> For the man who died so freely to save her life that day.
>   ("Utah Carroll")

> No more his silvery voice will ring, his spirit has gone to God.
> Around this spot let charity spring while we cover him with the sod.
>   ("The Burial of Wild Bill")

> The cowboy rose up sadly and mounted his little cayuse,
> Saying the time has come when longhorns and cowboys are no use.
> And while gazing sadly backwards upon the dead bovine,
> His broncho stepped in a dog hole and fell and broke his spine.
>   ("The Last Longhorn")[35]

The exemplar of these monodies is "Dixie Cowboy" (a.k.a. "When the
Work's All Done This Fall").[36] A group of jolly cowboys gathers round
to tell tales, and one of their number turns maudlin. He speaks of his
home in Dixie—"a good one too, you know"—and how he has not
returned for many years, but now, with the roundup nearly at an end,
he plans to go back—"I'm going to see my mother when the work's
all done this fall." That night, while riding guard on the herd, a storm
breaks and startles the cattle into a stampede; trying heroically to turn
the herd, his horse stumbles and "on to him did fall"—"Oh, he'll not
see his mother when the work's all done this fall."

The excessive sentimentality of these songs finds its equivalent in
the antebellum minstrel tunes of Stephen Foster. Other than the still-
familiar ballads—"My Old Kentucky Home," "Swanee River" (a.k.a.
Old Folks at Home)"—he also composed a handful of "mother" songs:
"Farewell, My Mother Dear," "Farewell, Sweet Mother," "A Dream of
My Mother and Home," and "Leave Me with My Mother." These quest-
ing sentiments for a mother who symbolizes home, security, strength,
and a nurturing selflessness—which, as the adult male sings, are lost
in the past (recoupable only as mawkish wistfulness)—resurface not
just in cowboy songs but across the range of material that old-time

musicians performed: "No One Loves You Any Better Than Your M-A-Double-M-Y," "You Will Never Miss Your Mother Until She Is Gone," "Whisper Your Mother's Name," "Mother, the Queen of My Heart," "If I Had Listened to My Mother," "Tell Mother I Will Meet Her," and, most poignantly, "If I Could Hear My Mother Pray Again."[37] The mother "left behind" became the key symbol in the creation of nostalgia (literally, a 'painful return') in old-time music—a universal trope that enabled the performer to intimate knowledge of personal loss with which his listeners could readily identify. The mother, like the old plantation South in Foster's songs, is a work of the imagination, existing only at the moment she is called forth—a palliative to alleviate the listener's anxieties. While the meaning of themes of mother and home may need little explication for the figure of the estranged cowboy, a more historically responsive explanation would place them in relation to the anxieties caused by modernity.

In musical terms ragtime and jazz embody the forms of cultural dissonance and are diametrically opposed to the themes of tradition and rootedness that sentimental and old-time music draw upon. In an article in *Seven Arts Magazine* in 1917 the journalist Hiram Moderwell writes: "I like to think that rag-time is the perfect expression of the American city, with its bustle and motion, its multitude of unrelated details, and its underlying rhythmic progress toward a vague somewhere. As you walk up and down the streets of an American city, you feel in its jerk and rattle, a personality different from that of any European capital. This is American. Rag-time, I believe, expresses it. It is today the one true American music."[38] If ragtime is the first popular musical expression of modernity, as Moderwell seems to suggest, with its blistering-hot rhythms expelled at tumultuous volume by five- and seven-piece ensembles, jazz intensified its effect. If ragtime was the "jerk and rattle" of a walk down the streets of a U.S. city, jazz was the whirl and oblivion of a speeding automobile ride. Writing in the *New York American* in 1917, a commentator suggests that "The Jazz, the most nervous of music, is wedded to one of the most erratic dances of the season."[39] The first jazz record, "Livery Stable Blues/Dixieland Jass Band One-Step" by the Original Dixieland Jazz Band, was released that year.[40] Three years later, while playing a successful tour of England, the group's leader, Nick LaRocca, gave eloquent voice to the new music's iconoclastic project: "Jazz is the assassination, the murdering, the slaying of syncopation. In fact, it is a revolution in this kind of music. . . . I even go so far as to confess we are musical anarchists. . . . Our prodigious outbursts are seldom consistent, every number played by us eclipsing in originality and effect our previous performance."[41] Cantwell neatly sums up this iconoclasm when he writes of early jazz that its "thick and explosive collective improvisation, fueled by the sounds of barrelhouse, brothels, and bandwagon, was a tribal bonfire in which all the sordid piety and vulgar sentimentality of bourgeois popular culture went up in smoke."[42] The apocryphal story of how Nick LaRocca came to leave England in fear for his life beautifully represents jazz music's attack on the "old order": "Reports that the cornetist [LaRocca] romanced with nearly every girl in London are grossly exaggerated, as he had time to meet only half of them. In fact, the tour of the Dixieland Band in England ended on a slightly sour note when an enraged Lord Harrington, father of one of London's most beautiful debutantes, chased the band down to the docks at Southampton with a loaded shotgun in his trembling hands."[43]

That jazz was a danger to the moral, if not social, fabric of the United States was obvious: "JAZZ RUINING GIRLS, DECLARES REFORMER" ran a 1922 headline in the *New York American*. "Moral disaster is coming to hundreds of young American girls through the pathological, nerve-irritating, sex-exciting music of jazz orchestras, according to the Illinois Vigilance Association. In Chicago alone the association's representatives have traced the fall of 1,000 girls in the last two years to jazz music."[44] Jazz was an easy scapegoat for this collective display of libido. Even Henry Ford, who laid claim to inventing the modern age, found it politically expedient to disparage jazz, apparently unconcerned with his far greater role in turning the world upside down. Peterson writes: "Rather than see the auto and mass production as having any part in the changes, [Ford] saw the problems as stemming from alcohol, tobacco use, and sexual license—all three fostered in the atmosphere created by jazz dancing."[45] Ford's solution was the reintroduction of older American pastimes. Through newspaper and magazine articles, guidebooks, radio, newsreel shorts, car dealerships, and competitions he led a crusade to bring back old-time fiddle music and square and round dancing, creating what Charles Wolfe considers a "flurry of popular interest in fiddlers and fiddling contests in 1925 and 1926."[46]

Ford's attempts to popularize older American styles of music and dance worked alongside the continued interest in rural music by the developing record companies. In 1927 Ralph Peer, now employed by the Victor Talking Machine Company to help it more fully exploit this market following its runaway success with Vernon Dalhart's "Wreck of the Old 97," set up a temporary recording studio in Bristol, Tennessee. Among the twenty-three artists he recorded during his stay were the two most important prewar country acts: the Carter Family and Jimmie Rodgers. A one-time railroad employee, Rodgers had turned to a career in music when tuberculosis made it impossible for him to hold down a regular job. At the auditions Peer was impressed enough with Rodgers's style to ask him to record two numbers but with the proviso that he perform older songs, or at least older-sounding songs that Peer could copyright and publish through his own company (Southern Music Publishing Company). Rodgers chose "The Soldier's Sweetheart"—a dirge popular during World War I—and a nineteenth-century vaudeville number, "Sleep, Baby, Sleep."[47] In his recordings Rodgers would soon expand upon this sentimental base, giving more time to developing his stage persona as a rounder, someone who makes the "rounds of criminal or disreputable resorts and activities," "a tough or dissolute idler."[48]

Rodgers's significance is related to the manner in which he transcended the strictures of old-time music.[49] By conjoining two distinct styles of address, Rodgers's routine effaced accusations of atavistic sentiment by straddling the past and present. In this sense it is important not to overstate the purity or the newness of jazz but to consider its own origins in other musical forms. Commenting on the Original Dixieland Jazz Band's first release, "Livery Stable Blues," the musicologist David Schiff writes, "It is a primitive novelty that advertises its own crudeness, a 12-bar blues repeated over and over without variations but with carefully planted barnyard breaks. . . . The animal sounds are a kind of metaphor for the musical confusion—*but also explain it away.*"[50] If the musical mimicry of barnyard animals mitigates the performance's restless propulsion into modernity, other jazz numbers of the period by black *and* white bands echoed this retrogressive act: Jelly Roll Morton's "Billy Goat Stomp" and the minstrel gags used in the spoken introductions to pieces like "Sidewalk Blues"; titles such as "Zulu's Ball" by King Oliver's Creole Jazz Band that recall a blackface minstrel tradition, as do the vocals by Walter Pichon on Oliver's 1929 recording of "I've Got That Thing," or Hoagy Carmichael's excessive blackface vocalizing on his hit "Rockin' Chair" (1930); and, not the least, in Cab Calloway's and Louis Armstrong's extravagant play with minstrelsy.[51] If some jazz kept a hesitant hold on the past, Rodgers too used the creative conflict between rural music and modernity to produce innovative music.

One element that set Rodgers apart from other old-time musicians was his singing. One of the many musicians directly influenced by Rodgers was Jimmie Davis, who noted, "Jimmie Rodgers had the best diction of anyone I ever knew."[52] Though Rodgers sang with a marked southern accent and at the top end of his range, unlike rural musicians such as Dock Boggs or Frank Hutchison, he forsook a raw regional twang.[53]

Just fourteen months after his debut recording session, Rodgers was augmenting his sound with cornet and clarinet accompaniment, giving distinct jazz inflections to "My Carolina Sunshine Girl" and "Blue Yodel #4" (1928). In February 1929 he was recording with an orchestra conducted by Leonard Joy that was comprised of piano, violin, cornet, clarinet, tuba, and traps. Later sessions would use the talents of Bob Sawyer's Jazz Band, Lani McIntire's Hawaiians, the Louisville Jug Band, the black blues guitarist Clifford Gibson, and, notably in July 1930, a session with Lillian and Louis Armstrong. At this session Rodgers recorded "Blue Yodel #9." It was typical Rodgers blues but powered here by Lillian's barrelhouse piano and punctuated by Louis's searing trumpet calls.

Like so many of Rodgers's songs, the lyrics are a collection of "found" blues stanzas. A police officer apprehends his character, who has been loafing about. Asked for his name, he replies: "You'll find my name on the tail of my shirt, / I'm a Tennessee hustler, I don't have to work." The song gives fair warning to other rounders to stay clear of his women and ends with his "good gal" walking into a joint with a .44 in each hand, saying: "Stand aside all you women and men, 'cos I'm looking for my man." This display of youthful braggadocio proved immensely popular with a new generation of musicians who sought to capitalize on the increased opportunities from radio and records for establishing a fully professional musical career.

As the market continued to expand for rural music (hillbilly and rural records accounted for 25 percent of the sixty-five million records sold in 1929), businessmen like Peer turned away from "field" recordings and began to secure the talents of professional performers who could deliver new material performed in Rodgers's hybrid style.[54] One pretender to Rodgers's crown was the young Gene Autry. Like Rodgers, Autry had worked for the railroad and had begun his musical career playing tent and medicine shows throughout the South. But unlike Rodgers, no one "discovered" Autry at a field recording audition. Aware that the opportunities for advancement in music lay in the big

metropolitan areas where the record and radio companies were centered, Autry headed for New York. Under the guidance of two similarly transplanted Oklahomans, Frankie and Johnny Marvin, Autry
found work with the American Record Corporation and Victor and
would make the odd recording, generally using a pseudonym, for a
number of other labels. He eventually signed an exclusive contract with
American Record.

During 1928–29 Autry had performed as Oklahoma's "Yodeling
Cowboy" on Tulsa's KVOO; for his first release he dropped the desig-
nation "Oklahoma," but "Yodeling Cowboy" remained fixed to his
name. However, at his initial American Record session in October
1929, Autry did not record cowboy songs; instead he turned in an
imitation of Jimmie Rodgers's "Blue Yodel #5" and a cover of Carson
Robison's hit "Left My Gal in the Mountains."[55] American Record spe
cialized in twenty-five-cent and three-for-a-dollar records distributed
principally through mail-order catalogs; it tailored a large part of its
"budget" releases for the rural market. "Blue Yodel #5" was the first of
more than twenty covers of Rodgers's songs that Autry would record.
Though Autry clearly had an affinity for Rodgers's music, the rather
more prosaic explanation for this mimicry was that Rodgers's Victor
releases sold at a premium. Buying an Autry release would give a cus-
tomer a Rodgers sound-alike at a rock bottom price. Furthermore, as
the country music archivist and historian Ronnie Pugh has noted,
Ralph Peer, Rodgers's publisher, supplied Autry with prerelease recordings of Rodgers; Peer obviously saw this as a way of increasing royal-
ties, irrespective of how damaging Autry's budget releases may have
been to the sales of his client's records.[56]

Regardless of the commercial imperative that lay behind many of
Autry's early recordings, he produced a significant body of work in this
period—many of the records that Autry made for American Record
and Victor between 1929 and 1933 were superlative examples of the
blue yodel idiom. Thus, though Autry was essentially imitative of Rodgers, Autry's apprenticeship formed the basis for his definitive synthesis
of the master's blue yodel and a more concerted exploitation of the
cowboy persona.

Working cowboys did not yodel, unless they were Tyrolean immigrants, aspiring blackface minstrels, or intent upon mimicking Jimmie
Rodgers's records. Rodgers's "blue yodel" was a further aspect of his
linking the past with the present, a way of taking rural music out of
antiquity and into the modern world. In giving the yodel a new context,

Jimmie Rodgers, "America's Blue Yodeler." The inscription suggests there is some substance to Autry's claims to have been a pal (or at least acquaintance) of Rodgers. (Photos provided courtesy of the Autry Qualified Interest Trust and the Autry Foundation. © 2001 by the Autry Qualified Interest Trust and the Autry Foundation.)

Rodgers gave it new meaning. Discussing Cliff Carlisle, yet another of Rodgers's many imitators, the country and blues writer Mark Humphries suggests that the blue yodel was an "appealing facade through which to vent sexual desire and aggression, stirrings which could be safely voiced in this new popular musical/poetic form, the blue yodel. At best, the yodel was more than a comic tag: it was a non-verbal statement of youthful bravado, a catharsis, Whitman's 'barbaric yawp.'"[57] The archetype of the white boy howling into a microphone, which the music critic Greil Marcus suggests was an image crucial to rock 'n' roll—"the sexy, half-crazed fool standing on the stage singing his guts out"—was earlier rehearsed by Rodgers and his blue yodeling acolytes (though it actually goes much further back, to the first blackface acts, and extends beyond rock 'n' roll, to be once more "reinvented" as punk rock).[59]

Touring troupes of Tyrolean musicians who performed in nineteenth-century vaudeville had brought Alpine yodeling to the United States, and it was a novel attraction competing with the other variety acts. Frank Norris introduced his middle-class readers to the wonders of turn-of-the-century vaudeville in a comic passage in *McTeague*. The entertainment for the evening consisted of an orchestra, "the Gleasons, in their mirth-making musical farce," "the Lamont Sisters . . . serio-comiques and skirt dancers," followed by a "great array of other 'artists' and 'specialty performers,' musical wonders, acrobats, lightning artists, ventriloquists, and last of all, 'The feature of the evening, the crowning scientific achievement of the nineteenth century, the kinetoscope.'"[59] The "artists" and "specialty performers" that most entrance Norris's characters are, first, a blackface musical ensemble "who seemed to be able to wrestle a tune out of almost anything—glass bottles, cigar-box fiddles, strings of sleigh-bells, even graduated brass tubes, which they rubbed with resined fingers. McTeague was stupefied with admiration."[60] Second, a band of German yodelers: "Three young women and a young man who played a zither occupied the stage. They were dressed in Tyrolese costume; they were yodlers, and sang in German about 'mountain tops' and 'bold hunters' and the like. The yodling chorus was a marvel of flute-like modulations. The girls were really pretty, and were not made up in the least. Their 'turn' had a great success. Mrs. Sieppe was entranced."[61] The appropriation of yodeling by blackface minstrels as a further novelty to add to their musical cacophony was not such a great leap. In fact, the music writer Nick Tosches argues that the crossover had occurred midway through the nineteenth century when the minstrel Tom Christian first popularized yodeling. By the turn of the century, yodeling, like banjo playing, had become part of college glee club repertoires.[62] However, the students and minstrels' yodels were little more than parodies of the Tyroleans' and were not blue yodels.

Rodgers's blue yodel was peerless, but it did not appear fully formed and without lineage from his disease-wracked lungs. When Rodgers chose to display his yodeling talent on "Sleep, Baby, Sleep" for his first recording session for Peer, he was following an arrangement, whether he was aware of it or not, that George P. Watson had recorded in 1911.[63] In his review of prewar blackface yodeling, Tosches notes that Matt Keefe had sung and yodeled the same song "since at least 1904, when he sang it with the Lew Dockstader troupe."[64] In 1908, when Keefe was performing in a Cohan and Harris Minstrels program, he was billed as a singer of "yodle songs." By the mid-1920s yodeling was an established element in blackface minstrelsy, whose foremost exponent was Emmett Miller. Since 1974 Tosches has sought to establish a space for Miller in the pantheon of American vernacular artists. Tosches's journey of discovery has been long and winding, filled with dead ends and wild flights of imagination, but the case he makes for Miller's artistry is compelling and worth quoting at length:

> The alchemy of Emmett Miller's music is as startling today as it was when he wrought it. Definable neither as country nor as blues, as jazz nor as pop, as black nor as white, but as both culmination and transcendence of these bloodlines and more, that alchemy, that music, stands as one of the most wondrous emanations, a birth-cry really, of the many-faced and one souled chimera of all that has come to be called American music. The very concept of him—a white man in blackface, a hillbilly singer and a jazz singer both, a son of the deep South and a roué of Broadway—is at once unique, mythic, and a perfect representation of the schizophrenic heart of what this country, with a straight face, calls its culture.[65]

Some of the preeminent jazz musicians of the day backed Miller on his late 1920s recordings for the Okeh label: Tommy and Jimmy Dorsey, Joe Tarto, Eddie Lang, Gene Krupa, and Jack Teagarden. These musicians gave a surprising contemporaneity to the minstrel skits that introduce many of the numbers and to the lazy slurring of vowels that was a mainstay of recorded minstrel singing. But more surprising and startling is his yodeling, which is blue in intent and effect—the yodel modulating around and on flattened sevenths, otherwise known as blue notes. His voice rises and falls with such rapidity and grace that the effect is both wretched and wondrous: "an expressiveness pure and free," writes Tosches. "We call it yodeling only because there is no other word for it."[66]

Jimmie Rodgers's music was steeped in minstrel influences. Early in his career he had performed in blackface, and he later recorded a blackface skit, but he did not sing in the minstrel style. Gene Autry, however, provided a fine example of minstrel singing on two songs recorded in late 1929, "Slu-Foot Lou"—"she's nine-foot-two"—and "Stay away from My Chicken House"—"or I'll cut you down Mexican style, I've got a long keen razor and a bulldog too. / You'll never look like nothin' when I get through with you." Late nineteenth- and early twentieth-century "coon songs" echo such imagery ad nauseam.[67] Rodgers billed himself as "America's Blue Yodeler" and "The Singing Brakeman," but these were only two of the personas he assumed during his short career; urbane balladeer, rounder, hobo, and cowboy were others.

The opportunity afforded to rural musicians to slip in and out of identities was a significant reason why so many young men like Rodgers sought a public platform as performers. Though Rodgers dressed in cowboy duds for a photo session, he recorded only seven cowboy songs; this identity seems to have had less imaginative hold on him than the more contemporary rounder persona. In this play with identity Rodgers was doing the same as many other young contemporary musical performers. The West Virginian and former miner Frank Hutchison (whom Tony Russell rightly claims dominates the first chapter in any history of hillbilly blues) did not record cowboy songs. Nevertheless, he posed as a cowboy for an utterly charming photographic portrait. He is wearing a cocked, small-brimmed cowboy hat, neckerchief, white shirt, long leather wrist bands (like "Broncho Billy" Anderson), cartridge belt and holster holding an automatic pistol, and a pair of sheepskin chaps. Clasped somewhat incongruously to his chest is a puppy or small dog whose wiry hair matches the wool of the chaps. The photograph contrasts with the more commonly published image of Hutchison as an earnest young musician—suited, seated, and staring directly into the camera. Here he looks nervous and uneasy, belying the composure and confidence in the way he sings and plays guitar.[68]

The play with persona offered a particular romantic distraction and, if lucky and gifted enough, escape from the workaday toil of a miner or railroad man. For this reason the hobo persona, which competes with the cowboy as an "occupation" free from immediate responsibility to work and family, proved alluring to musicians and their audiences. Cowboy songs and hobo songs offer the same set of sentiments: celebration of a life lived free and easy but also one suffused with nostalgic regret for mothers and sweethearts left behind. Dying hoboes are as common as dying cowboys in these songs. Hoboes and cowboys may wander, but they always think of home. The freedom implied in their lifestyle is limited, and eventually they must pay the price. The miners or railroad workers, whose fantasies of escape from the humdrum are evoked by these songs, also are reassured that they have made the right decision in staying home, working, and raising a family.

However, the stability of family and home was historically under threat. The migration of rural workers to urban-industrial jobs echoed the themes of fugitive restlessness and separation from kinfolk in cowboy and hobo songs. When Gene Autry left New York for Chicago in late 1931, he was following a route (albeit rather convolutedly) that many other Oklahomans and southerners had traveled since the end of World War I. "Figures from the 1930 census show," writes Cantwell, that "roughly one-tenth of the Indiana urban population, and one-twentieth of the Illinois urban population, had been born in the middle South."[69] From the early 1930s to the mid-1940s Chicago was thought to hold the greatest concentration of musicians playing in a rural idiom.[70] Autry had moved to Chicago for an engagement with the radio station WLS (World's Largest Store), which Sears Roebuck had once owned but sold to the *Prairie Farmer* newspaper in 1928.[71] The station's principal audience, according to Cantwell, were rural midwesterners, but the range of the station's signal went beyond that region. Autry had his own morning show on WLS, *Conqueror Record Time,* where he boosted sales of his own and other Conqueror records. He also had an increasingly lucrative contract with the Sears catalog through which he endorsed various products and by which Conqueror records were distributed and sold. Autry also had a featured spot on the highly popular WLS show *The National Barn Dance.* Though he had gone to Chicago to build upon his success with a maudlin mountain ballad—"That Silver-Haired Daddy of Mine," which would eventually sell more than a million copies—he now, with radio backing, began more fully and consistently to exploit a cowboy identity. The growing importance of commercial sponsorship in maintaining a radio presence supported this process.

Following the relaxation of advertising restrictions in the early 1930s, as the radio historian Michele Hilmes notes, "sponsored programs came to dominate the airwaves."[72] "Programs," she continues, "were created with the specific idea of attracting sponsors, not of providing a high-minded public service."[73] In 1932, when the NBC network picked up the *National Barn Dance* and aired it nationally on Saturday nights, promoting a rural or down-home character (which would also boost sales of advertised goods) was crucial in maintaining the program's viability. The figure of the cowboy assumed a significant role in this process. Paradoxically, this figure rooted in history also presented a modern, yet uncontroversial, persona. Old-time music suggested a parochial and atavistic outlook on life. It was not readily adaptable as a marketing image for products that wanted to suggest modernity, albeit of the unthreatening kind. In contrast to the hobo, rounder, and hillbilly figures that competed for prominence, the cowboy proved much more acceptable to sponsors. The increasing role played by sponsorship determined that radio advertising, performing, and song content were compatible with economic interests. In this respect Jimmie Rodgers's rounder figure fell outside the sponsors' conception of their audience.

Rodgers included a number of risqué and morally suspect songs in his repertoire. The memoir of his wife, Carrie Rodgers, reveals:

> In blue brakie garb, including the peaked cap, the blue bandanna and the watch and chain, Jimmie Rodgers, boyishly slender and unassuming, gave to the patrons of the Earle [theater] his "T for Texas" and "Soldier's Sweetheart," together with other numbers. For his encore he gave—"Frankie and Johnny"!
>
> In those days you didn't sing "Frankie and Johnny" in polite society nor in public to a mixed audience. So—Jimmie Rodgers did.
>
> You sang it in furtive places, with a dropped eyelid and insinuating innuendoes. So—Jimmie Rodgers didn't.
>
> He gave it to the Earle with exactly the same earnestness, the same heart-throb sympathy that he had put into "Soldier's Sweetheart."[74]

Rodgers's audience clearly enjoyed his good-humored slights to the mores and conventions of more morally uptight citizens. If his rounder persona gave them access to déclassé public spaces such as bars and brothels, as in "Frankie and Johnny" or "Gambling Bar Room Blues," other songs opened the private space of the bedroom, as in "Let Me Be Your Sidetrack" or "Long Tall Mama Blues." The singers who followed the trail of Rodgers's blue yodel took this kind of sexual innuendo to new heights of ribaldry and masculine posturing.

Cliff Carlisle was particularly adroit at this genre. In "That Nasty Swing" Carlisle uses a phonographic metaphor to proclaim his sexual potency: "Wind my motor, honey—I've got a double spring, / Put the needle in the groove and do that nasty swing." But the master of this form was the Louisiana governor-to-be, Jimmie Davis, whose early 1930s recordings, such as "Red Nightgown Blues," "Tom Cat and Pussy Blues" ("You oughta seen that cock and pussy"), "Bear Cat Mama from Horner's Corners," "Wampus Kitty Mama," "High-Geared Mama," and "Good Time Papa Blues," are filled with tales of hot mamas and hard papas. While bawdy songs were fine in the confines of the home when played on a phonograph, or played live to a paying audience, they were totally unacceptable to radio sponsors and no doubt to a large segment of radio's ever-growing constituency.

Autry too recorded his share of "mama and papa" blues in the early 1930s: "Birmingham Daddy," "Bear Cat Papa Blues," "Wildcat Mama Blues," "High Steppin' Mama Blues," and "Do Right Daddy Blues." But on "The Rheumatism Blues" his carousing days are over—his double spring has snapped: "I've got that old rheumatism and I'm left alone, / My baby's found a daddy with a strong backbone." Jimmie Davis, who sang about a similar enervating complaint on "Organ Grinder Blues," had the protagonist of his song seek out the monkey-gland cure that was then being plugged on the semilegitimate Mexican border stations whose powerful transmitters covered much of the South.[75]

Border radio, which used Mexico's laissez-faire attitude toward granting radio licenses to circumvent the oligopoly of NBC, AT&T, and CBS, sold airspace to anyone willing to pay the price, regardless of intent and credibility. Radio evangelists joined the airwaves with quacks—who promised cancer cures or potency revivers in the form of goat or monkey-gland transplants—alongside other contemporary medicine show–style hucksters. The legitimate radio barn dances, which potentially shared the same audience, found it particularly important to differentiate themselves. At the end of 1934, when the notoriously metropolitan-centric showbiz journal *Variety* finally took note of the huge audiences that the barn dances drew, it was careful also to note that these shows did not, nor did they need to, solicit patent medicine sponsorship.[76]

Since the inception of *The National Barn Dance* in 1926, virtually every radio station that laid claim to a rural audience used the same basic Saturday night variety formula first tried and tested in Chicago on WLS. By Charles Wolfe's tally 137 stations in the South and Southwest had such a program by 1932; only 45 had made affiliations with the national broadcasting networks. Those that did not have a link-up produced their own budget versions of barn dances.[77] According to *Variety:*

> No other type of program has built such a loyal audience and no other type has continued to remain a top radio attraction through the years of broadcasting. And at present no other program is so completely sponsored as barn dances. Advertisers have swung sharply to the Saturday night clod-hopping festivals until at present it is practically impossible to get advertising space on the barn dances as operated over WLS, WSM [*Grand Ole Opry*], WHO [Des Moines], WFAA-WBAP [Ft. Worth], KSL [*Utah Rodeo*, Salt Lake City], KVOO [Tulsa], KTHS [Hot Springs, Arkansas], WBT [Charlotte, N.C.].[78]

Barn dances generally played before an audience (both the *National* and the *Opry* used auditoriums), and although the format varied slightly from station to station, all used the same basic formula. A master of ceremonies introduced the acts—a variety of musical and comedy turns—and instilled a sense of order on what appeared to be an otherwise informal and unchoreographed flow of "performers working in and out of the show as it goes along."[79] Cantwell argues that the basic presentation owed much to the format of the earlier blackface minstrel shows, "substituting painted barn beams, hayricks, rail fences, and the like for the minstrel show's cabin, cotton patch, levee, and riverboat and costuming [the] performers—tradesmen and artisans who had at first appeared at the studio in business suits—in overalls, straw hats, kerchiefs, and the like."[80] The minstrel show emcee acted as an interlocutor who, as the cultural historian W. T. Lhamon Jr. notes, "began every show addressing the endmen with the exasperated dictum: 'Gentlemen, be seated!' From the beginning to the end of each individual show . . . the minstrel show has displayed struggle over the seating of chaotic energy."[81] The barn dances retained this idea of a barely contained energy. And they featured blackface entertainers along with the minstrel show semicircle, which "drew the audience into a closed social 'circle' with the troupe."[82]

Though the *Opry* did not use the semicircle of performers—unlike most other shows, as *Variety* notes, the *Opry* allowed each "act ten or fifteen minutes in which to do its stint and then goes on to the next act"—Autry worked with the format at WLS and later adopted it for his own stage shows.[83] The country music historian Douglas B. Green writes: "The entire cast, including Autry, was present on stage throughout the full performance, seated on chairs in a semicircle well behind

Yodeling cowboy Gene Autry, surrounded by unidentified minstrel troupe ca. 1932. (Photos provided courtesy of the Autry Qualified Interest Trust and the Autry Foundation. © 2001 by the Autry Qualified Interest Trust and the Autry Foundation.)

whoever was in the limelight at any given time."[84] That blackface minstrelsy had a huge influence on vernacular and mainstream American music is not in doubt, but just as important is its effect on the presentation of self and community as featured in the singing cowboy films of the 1930s. Its lack of visibility is due to the performance and construction of race, as evinced in the figure of the cowboy, who from the early 1930s to late 1940s would dominate the presentation of rural music in the United States.

For young performers like Autry a professional career in music offered not only money and fame but also the opportunity to assume the romantic aura of the musician as an outsider—a renegade cut loose from the moral restraints of his culture—a condition that Cantwell beautifully evokes: "The musician lingers on the moral edge of rural society not only because he is an idler, then, or because he may be strange in some way—blind, perhaps, or vaguely effeminate—but because his music opens a door onto unacted desires and may be a sign in him of daemonic energies which can also find an outlet in destructive or antisocial conduct, energies which it is the business of morality to subdue or of religion to harness."[85] The musician's liminality is what made him both marketable *and* potentially unmarketable. Positioned too far outside his community's values and interests, he could become a threat rather than a figure acting out the limits of permissible behavior (as exemplified in Carrie Rodgers's account of her husband singing "Frankie and Johnny"). Too great a reduction of the distance between the artist and his audience, however, would produce a banality that commercial interests, which relied on the sponsored musician's distinctiveness, could not successfully exploit. The performer functioned as a symbol of individualism that market interests knowingly exploited in the process of individuating their products. In her superb essay "'We Always Tried to Be Good People': Respectability, Crazy Water Crystals, and Hillbilly Music on the Air, 1933–35," the historian Pamela Grundy examines how many hillbilly (by the late 1920s this was the most commonly used industry term for rural music) musicians walked this "fine line between acceptability and censure." "By the 1930s, the range of acceptable behavior had narrowed considerably," she argues. "Shows composed of songs that posed direct challenges to social hierarchies would probably have had an extremely short life in an industry that depended on business sponsorship for its survival; programs that offered only palliatives for difficulties too harsh to ignore would probably have had less appeal. . . . Musicians, who negotiated a cultural ground where the backgrounds and concerns of a wide variety of individuals could seem to meet, managed to avoid both fates."[86]

The personae offered by rural vernacular performance—old time (such as the Carter Family), rounder (Jimmie Rodgers), folk singer–mountaineer (Bradley Kincaid), hobo (Goebel Reeves), or hillbilly (Carson Robison)—had their positive selling points, but they also had negatives. Old-time and folk music suggested tradition and stability, but this type of music lay outside modernity. Rounder and hobo suggested a romantic disengagement with everyday concerns, but their appeal to men placed them too far outside the sphere of the feminine; their antidomesticity negated their usefulness to advertisers who sought the approval of women as the principal consumers of branded goods. The figure of the hillbilly, who combines the character traits of old time, folk, rounder, and hobo, carried far too many negative connotations to make him into a dynamic commercial symbol that could serve the needs of a wide range of sponsors seeking a national audience.

The historian Richard White has noted how the cultural and social stigma attached to white working-class southerners—whom the hillbilly musician represented and to a great extent symbolized—became particularly pronounced with the migration of "Okies" to California during the depression: "Many of them had left the South to avoid being reduced to doing 'niggers' work,' but this loyalty to southern values only fed a second source of scorn: a general disdain for poor white southerners, the 'poor white trash' of regional stereotypes."[87] James N. Gregory, a historian of the Okie migration, notes that the explanation for this stereotype took, first, "a close association with the heavily stigmatized occupation of farm laborer, and second, association with the equally stigmatized background of Southern sharecropper. These were elements out of which the Okie stereotype emerged. . . . Class was the essential dividing line."[88] The stigma attached to rural labor and customs was not limited to southern migrants in California but was apparent earlier in the century in southern towns, as Grundy notes: "Beginning in the late nineteenth century, writings that ranged from accomplished novels to the doggerel verse published in small-town newspapers began to shift from accounts of stalwart yeoman farmers to portraits of laughable bumpkins, unfamiliar with city ways. Textile industry spokesmen provided particularly harsh critiques, in part because ideas of rural backwardness provided a convenient way to deflect criticisms of mill village conditions."[89]

As a national figure, the cowboy evaded the pejorative connotations attached to the idea of the South cut adrift from the rest of the nation while still appearing to represent an image of regionalism that escaped accusations of atavistic parochialism. While the figure of the hillbilly retained the signs of an overdetermined class system, the cowboy suggested classlessness. If the hillbilly suggested a South forever stalled at the frontier of modernity, the cowboy suggested a figure able to transverse this imposing boundary without the fear of losing his identity to the forces of urbanization and factory wage labor. The figures of the hobo or rounder suggested an unrestrained masculinity; the cowboy, however, was able to move with ease between the domestic space defined as feminine and the homosocial public sphere. While the white southerner retained the association with an unbridled racism, the cowboy maintained an uncontroversial image of white supremacy. This was evident in the absence or utter marginalization of blacks in fictions of the West and the subjugation of the native and Mexican populations.

Dislocated rural southerners carried with them the negative attributes of poverty, class, overt racism, regionalism, anachronistic work practices, and lack of sophistication. Southern vernacular music paradoxically confirmed this identity, yet it also displayed a remarkable ability to adapt and respond to a diversity of influences. No artist showed this more effectively than Rodgers. Rodgers's forte was in recording and in live performances. However, when he died in May 1933, the depression had greatly affected the sales of records, and radio had become the dominant medium for the transmission of rural music. NBC started broadcasting *The National Barn Dance* nationally the year before Rodgers died, and it is debatable whether Rodgers's overt proletarian appeal would have secured the same sponsorship deals that Autry—Rodgers's one-time imitator and now eulogizer (Autry recorded four tributes to Rodgers)—enjoyed.[90]

Because Autry was an early morning performer on *Conqueror Record Time*, his principal audience was female. As Grundy notes, "Women made up a large and vocal segment of the hillbilly audience."[91] Furthermore, as Michelle Hilmes records, women made up the majority of radio listeners, period. Women ranged "from 55–60 percent at night to more than 70 percent in the daytime—and the purchase of products by women provided its most basic economic support."[92] Thus Autry addressed his now stabilized cowboy persona to his female constituency. Though he would continue to record songs outside the cowboy genre, the bawdy blues-based material disappeared, retained only in the blue yodel that, through his popularity over the radio, became fixed as a vocal motif of cowboy singing. Autry's first starring appearance in a feature film, *Tumbling Tumbleweeds* (Republic, 1935), introduced him in a domestic environment, not out riding the range, and his presence was announced by his singing off-screen "And yodel my troubles away." The initial focus on his voice delays his entrance from a room adjoining the parlor and plays with audience expectations, introducing him in a way that was familiar from his radio appearances: the disembodied voice of a cowboy crooner whose yodel no longer suggests a youthful boast but a congeniality and a contented accommodation with the world.

Other than Autry, the group that came to exemplify radio's exploitation of the singing cowboy was the Sons of the Pioneers. Formed around the nucleus of Leonard Slye (later Roy Rogers), Bob Nolan, Tim Spencer, and Hugh Farr, this southern California group began broadcasting from radio station KFWB in 1933. The group's extraordinary three- and four-part harmonies and the song-writing talents of

Nolan and Spencer further refined and polished the performance of cowboy songs. Just four years (1929–33) separate the recording of Dick Devall's two performances and the Sons of the Pioneers' early forays on wax, but it may as well be a thousand. I can think of no other shift within a popular musical form that is as strongly marked. Beyond the subject matter of dying cowboys, little links Devall and the Pioneers. Devall's coarse and untutored vocals sound as if his larynx was pickled in raw alcohol and tobacco juice; in contrast the Pioneers' vocals are genteel and refined—no sound is sweeter.

The 1998 release by Bear Family Records of the Pioneers' first recordings for the Standard Radio Transcription Company offers a unique review of the breadth of song styles and material performed by such cowboy-attired musicians in the early to mid-1930s.[93] The use of transcription discs (performances recorded exclusively for radio) allowed stations to work around record companies' refusal to allow their recordings to be played on the air. However, radio stations could buy licenses that allowed them access to the recorded libraries of the various transcription services. Designed as folios of popular songs that would have a long shelf life, the transcription discs are far better indicators of the rich musical tradition upon which the performers drew than their recordings for commercial record labels, which were conceived as novelties in search of large sales.

Outside the traditional and recently composed cowboy songs, nineteenth-century minstrel songs make by far the largest contribution to the Pioneers' repertoire. In part this was because the songs were no longer under copyright but also because audiences knew these songs. From the antebellum songs of Dan Emmett and Stephen Foster, such as "Jim Crack Corn" and "Old Black Joe," via spirituals such as "Dese Bones Gwine to Rise Again" and "coon songs" such as Harry Von Tilzer's "Rufus Rastus Johnson Brown (What You Gonna Do When the Rent Comes 'Round)," through more contemporary minstrelsy such as Carson J. Robison's "Open Up Dem Pearly Gates" and Will Hays's "Cabin in the Lane," the Pioneers offered a veritable history lesson in minstrel tunes. That said, modernity did affect these songs. As with nineteenth-century British tunes such as "In the Gloaming," the Pioneers' arrangements ensure a contemporaneous setting through "jazzing" the breaks between verses and chorus. Indeed, perhaps their most adventurous arrangements are on the instrumentals, where Hugh Farr's fiddle takes the lead, particularly on such jazz numbers as Jelly Roll Morton's "Milenburg Joys" or W. C. Handy's "St. Louis Blues." Also performed are square dances, waltzes, and schottisches, mawkish nine-teenth-century tunes such as "When You and I Were Young, Maggie," yodel numbers (mostly Tyrolean), and a cover of Jimmie Rodgers's "Hadie Brown." The 151 songs that the band recorded for Standard between August 1934 and September 1935 represent probably the most melancholic collection of songs ever grouped together—death's hand lies heavily on the minds and tongues of this young band. It is as if all the sentimental Victorian sorrow ever wrought has here found its last and greatest expression—a memento mori shrouded in the most modern of vocal and instrumental arrangements. This is a pristine example of what I mean when I say the cowboy was a mediator between the old and the new.

In a feature item included in the press book for *Tumbling Tumbleweeds*, Autry explains his ambition to become the Stephen Foster of cowboy songs: "The musical taste of the country has drifted away from negro inspired music [minstrel tunes] and more and more we hear the songs of America's true pioneers." Nonetheless, the corpus of songs on which the Sons of the Pioneers drew suggests that minstrel and cowboy songs worked alongside each other, rather than the latter's super-seding the former. Away from the influences of the city, the cowboy, like his blackface minstrel cousin, acquired a "primitive philosophy." Autry adds his take on why so many express a melancholic sensibility: "All savage tribes eventually get this pessimistic viewpoint which seems native to those who are close to the soil. In the American cowboy it expresses itself in their songs, and they develop a plaintive music which is now considered characteristic of these roaming westerners. . . . It's not exactly a negative philosophy, because in expressing dissatisfaction with sad things there is a natural approval of happier moods."[94]

While Autry and the Sons of the Pioneers were establishing their radio cowboy personas, Broadway was discovering the appeal of cowboy songs. Billy Hill, a new composer, wrote one of the most popular songs of 1933. "He had been trying for a long time to sell his cowboy song, and it was only when Joe Morrison began to sing it at New York's Paramount Theatre that it attracted attention," Spaeth recounts. "There was no love interest in 'The Last Round-Up' (except for the horse), but the sincerity of its sentiment and individual handling of the melody, with a suggestion of distant trumpets and a direct quotation from traditional cowboy material in the middle ('Git along, little dogies'), all combined to create a novel and highly interesting effect."[95] Hill's song began a cycle of popular cowboy tunes that owed little, beyond the odd quotation, to traditional or turn-of-the-century cowboy songs nor, at least initially, to the musical performance styles of radio cowboys. Recordings of "The Last Round-Up" sold more than 100,000 copies and, as the music business historians Russell Sanjek and David Sanjek note, "signaled a small upturn in industry income, the first since 1929."[96] Autry recorded one of the earliest versions in October 1933. Hill continued to have hits during the next few years and continued to exploit the field of cowboy songs, notably with "Empty Saddles." The popularity of cowboy tunes reached something of a plateau in 1936 when Johnny Mercer gently spoofed the form with "I'm an Old Cowhand," a massive hit for Bing Crosby. Hill's cowboy songs, as well as Mercer's, would soon join the corpus of work upon which radio, recording, and film cowboys (and cowgirls) would draw.

When Gilbert Seldes reviewed the state of popular music in 1924, cowboy songs were barely a historical footnote; about twelve years later they were being sung across the spectrum of American music. After the transition to sound, Hollywood, in its use of popular song and through its links to the music publishing, radio, and recording industries, had a significant role to play in the apparently universal popular appeal of cowboy music.

FOUR

Cowboy Republic: Producing
the Singing Western

From the 1910s until the late twenties, westerns played a significant
role in the production schedules of most of Hollywood's larger studios.
The extent of the major studios' investment in the genre was such that
independent and Poverty Row studios focused their production energies elsewhere. Following the transition to sound, however, the majors
reduced their involvement in the production of series westerns and
terminated their contracts with their leading western stars. The continued demand for western films, the availability of talent, and the lack
of competition from the major studios provided an opportunity for
independent and Poverty Row studios to produce westerns. These
companies, often lacking in resources and underfinanced, maintained
a flow of western films to independent rural, small-town, and urban
neighborhood theaters. However, it was not until the formation in
1935 of Republic Pictures that the studios could guarantee a greater
degree of quality and consistent distribution to exhibitors, whose patrons appeared to have an insatiable appetite for westerns.

With Hollywood's move to sound production, the western foundered. The initial technical demands of sound meant that the studios needed to produce films within a tightly controlled studio environment, which ruled out westerns, though the industry was still producing silent westerns for theaters that had yet to convert to sound. However, by 1929 most major studios had abandoned silent films, and they had overcome technical difficulties involving location sound recording. Fox returned to producing westerns with *In Old Arizona* (1929) and Paramount with *The Virginian* (1929). Both films were box office successes. In part, these properties proved attractive to their respective companies because they reinvigorated the fading novelty of sound by emphasizing a nonstudio environment, but independent exhibitors also had been clamoring for western films.

Independent exhibitors formed one pressure group that was pushing the government to take antitrust action against the major studios for restraint of trade. In particular, these exhibitors felt aggrieved because of the studios' imposition of blind and block booking. In effect, this policy meant that exhibitors were obliged to book a block of films unseen—hence, "blind"—regardless of quality or their patrons' preferences, in order to secure the more desirable titles that the studios offered. This meant that rural and small-town exhibitors would have to show films that their audience often found distasteful, particularly those films that had characters that were immoral or, at least, amoral. Films that had played to appreciative audiences in first-run metropolitan theaters were not guaranteed a similar reception in small-town and rural America. This was why Harry Brandt, president of the Independent Theatre Owners of America, released his infamous 1938 list of leading female stars—Katharine Hepburn, Joan Crawford, Greta Garbo, Marlene Dietrich—who were "box office poison." Nevertheless, because the major studios realized the majority of their income from the first-run metropolitan theaters where the stars were popular, they continued to produce "sophisticated urban dramas" and obliged independent exhibitors to rent them.

In 1927 the government finally began to take action against the major studios' monopolistic practices. As one means of trying to assuage independent exhibitors, the major studios made an effort to meet their demands by producing westerns that they hoped would play to equally positive reactions in the major cities and the smallest towns. Furthermore, in addition to producing prestige westerns, such as *The Big Trail* (Fox, 1930), *The Painted Desert* (Pathé, 1931), *Billy the Kid*

(MGM, 1930), and *Cimarron* (RKO, 1931), some studios began new series westerns. However, the studios' placatory attitude toward the demands of the independent sector was short lived. Prestige westerns were extraordinarily expensive yet did poor box-office business. With the huge debts they had incurred from investing in sound technology and overexpansion in real estate and theater acquisition, the major film companies retrenched and concentrated their resources on films produced in the studio and aimed primarily to secure the patronage of the metropolitan movie goer.

The evident decline in western productions between 1931 and 1935 reflects the transition to sound and the pragmatic strategies that the studios used to ameliorate the consequences of a crippled national economy.[1] While economizing did not mean that the major studios completely abandoned series westerns, they canceled contracts with the older cohort of western stars. In their place they hired less expensive actors who were new to the genre and who offered youthful contrast to the superannuated old guard. Young bloods included George O'Brien at Fox, Tom Keene at RKO, Randolph Scott at Paramount, and, for a series of six films, John Wayne at Warner Bros. Despite such pragmatic cost cutting, however, the big studios found it impossible to reduce their budgets to the meager levels at which Poverty Row productions operated. The film historian Paul Seale writes: "Paying bottom dollar for everything, the Poverty Row producer could turn out a film for as little as $3,000 (though often closer to $10,000 or $15,000, still one tenth the budget of a low-budget major film), calculated to return its costs and a small profit in distribution."[2] Drawing on information reported by *Variety*, Seale notes that before 1928 "the chief producers of Westerns were the major companies and larger independents: Paramount, Universal, First National, Fox, FBO, and Pathé. The smaller independents avoided Westerns because of the formidable competition."[3] Faced with the financial demands of prestige westerns and unable to match the skeletal economies of the Poverty Row producers, major studio productions of westerns were stagnating by 1932.

The availability of older western stars aided the independent sector's exploitation of the genre. Tom Mix moved from Fox at the end of 1928 and was employed at FBO and Universal: he concluded his film career with an embarrassing role in the serial *The Miracle Rider* (1935) for Mascot. Equally, Mascot serials provided work for Harry Carey, who, already past his youthful best at forty, had earlier moved from Pathé to a brief starring stint at MGM, most notably in *Trader Horn*

(1931). After that, Carey starred in cheap budget productions by Art Class and Ajax/Commodore, then took supporting roles to Randolph Scott in Paramount's series adaptations of Zane Grey's novels. The careers of other silent western actors followed similar trajectories in descending from one of the five major studios to Poverty Row through the underresourced but aspiring Columbia and Universal. In 1929 Buck Jones moved from Fox to Beverly/Columbia, then to Universal in 1934, ending his career at Monogram. Tim McCoy, who was MGM's lone series western star, starred in a serial for Universal, then joined Buck Jones at Columbia, leaving in 1934. McCoy's film career ended with pictures for Puritan, Victory, PRC, and Monogram. In 1929 Ken Maynard crossed from First National to Universal with contracts at Tiffany and KBS/World Wide before returning to Universal in 1933. He too worked for Mascot, Columbia, and Grand National before finishing his career at Colony and Monogram.

The overall consequence of the shift in production from the majors to the low-budget producers was a demonstrably shoddier prod-

Harry Carey

Tim McCoy

uct. Independent exhibitors were vociferous in registering their complaints about the decline in quality. By 1934 the pages of the *Motion Picture Herald* carried their vocal campaign against the poor quality series western, which for many constituted their primary source of income: "The John Wayne Westerns at one time spelled B. O. for me, but it's impossible for anyone to make several pictures a year and make good ones and this one [*Rainbow Valley* (1935)] is a very weak sister."[4] Two other exhibitors criticized *Trail Beyond* (1934) as "terribly amateurish."[5] Wayne made both *Trail Beyond* and *Rainbow Valley*, series westerns, for Monogram. The Monogram films mark a distinct departure from those that Wayne had made for Warner Bros. and graphically illustrate the substance of the exhibitors' concerns. The Warner Bros. films demonstrated a variety of situations that embellished fundamental formulas; their story quality remained high because they were adaptions of successful narratives from Ken Maynard films. For example, *Haunted Gold* (1932) was a remake of *The Phantom City* (1928). A judicious use of stock footage (also taken from the relatively high-budget

Maynard silent series) worked to secure production values that were higher than usual. In contrast, exhibitors could barely differentiate the Monogram films. However, Monogram's inferior product was not simply the result of a lack of concern for aesthetics but was symptomatic of an independent sector that was underfinanced, irregular, and anarchic. To some degree the formation of Republic Pictures in 1935 consolidated this segment of the market and provided concomitant improvement in picture quality.

Republic was an amalgamation of Mascot, Liberty, Majestic, Chesterfield, and Monogram that emerged from Consolidated Laboratories, a film-processing corporation owned by Herbert J. Yates. Consolidated Laboratories had controlled the processing work for the expanding independent sector and was in a strong position to capitalize on the financial weakness of depression casualties. Yates forced independent companies in debt for unpaid processing contracts to cede control of their limited assets (including contract players such as Wayne) to Yates, who centralized film production and reorganized the distribution of films to independent exhibitors. In this way Republic effectively stabilized financial flows, and this in turn strengthened production planning. Behind the economic restructuring was the need to address the poor product quality widely associated with the low-budget independents that Yates had incorporated. The film historian Brian Taves underlines the significance of the new formation: "Unlike most of its immediate competitors, and because of its emergence from Consolidated Labs, Republic successfully mated low-budget material with a degree of polished Hollywood seamlessness never equaled by the other smaller studios."[6]

Initially, Republic announced a limited production schedule of twenty features and eight westerns. Republic clearly identified the western as a distinct product and kept its accounts for westerns' costs and revenues separate from its features. Republic would split its westerns equally between Gene Autry and John Wayne. By May 1935 Republic was responding to exhibitors' demands and increased its annual production to twenty-six features and sixteen westerns. The studio promoted its improvement in production values by announcing that it was "not aiming to make pictures for double-bills."[7] Because all films were double billed at the time, Republic's declaration was a signal to independent exhibitors of its intention to produce a quality product that they could sell on its merits. Republic used generic repositioning as part of its drive to dissociate itself from its shoddy predecessors; an advertisement in the trade press sold one of its films in the following manner: "Not a Western in the strict interpretation of that term, it is an outdoor, action-packed adventure yarn which carries a charming romantic contrast to its vibrant drama."[8]

Republic's efforts were recognized: the *Motion Picture Herald* agreed that the new Republic series had "better than ordinary production values. With John Wayne ranking as one of the foremost Western stars, his name looms as the outstanding commercial feature, but other qualities of the picture should not be ignored in its marketing."[9] Letters from exhibitors to the magazine supported this perception: "Here is a Western that is a Western. Cowboy singing, action, theme song, everything. Give it preferred time."[10]

Republic's phenomenal success with independent exhibitors (and in turn their audiences) led the studio to increase its production budget from $2 million to $9 million between 1935 and 1940. During World War II its production budget more than doubled, to $20 million.[11] Though Wayne's series and others such as the Three Mesquiteers' contributed hugely to the studio's success, Gene Autry's films were the primary source of Republic Pictures' fortune.

When Republic took over Mascot, it also took over Autry's initial film contract. Yates was also the head of Autry's recording company—American Record Corporation—and was responsible for orchestrating Autry's career in recording, film, and radio. Yates exploited Autry's established reputation as a live performer and was in a unique position from which to synchronize Autry's film promotion with other dominant forms of popular media. Autry's first film appearance was in *In Old Santa Fe* (1934), a picture starring Ken Maynard, for Mascot, and its marketing explicitly identified the well-known public profile that Autry had gained through his music and radio work. Posters for the film billed Autry as "The World's Greatest Cowboy Singer" or as the "Cowboy Idol of the Air." Thus the marketing encouraged audiences to buy tickets to see someone with whom they were already familiar. In this film and in all his subsequent starring appearances, Gene Autry appeared as Gene Autry. Audiences were not initially paying to view an actor essaying a dramatic role but to see "Gene Autry—Radio Star." Just as he amalgamated a number of film studios under the banner of Republic Pictures, Yates had earlier consolidated his position in the phonograph industry by buying out Brunswick and Columbia records in the early 1930s. These companies now operated as subsidiaries of American Record, the leading supplier of records for the rural market as a result of the consolidation.[12] Autry, then, was a key link in a chain that held Yates's various media investments together. Therefore, it is not surprising that Autry's film "character" is often acutely self-reflexive, often appearing within the diegesis as a recording and radio star. However, the visual nature of cinema, together with its narrative form, meant that it could develop and expand the personality of Autry and other singing cowboys into something capable of richer, more complex meanings than radio could afford.

Historical and critical accounts of cinema that place film as the dominant medium of the twentieth century distort the picture of how people actually engaged with the variety of media available to them. For Autry, and no doubt for much of his audience, radio was at least an equally significant channel. Film worked alongside records, live performances, and radio. Autry commanded greater audience numbers through radio than he could ever hope to reach through the other media. Sponsorship deals and product endorsements ensured that radio, after establishing the networked *Melody Ranch* show in 1940, was his most lucrative engagement. Although he did not have his own radio show after leaving WLS in 1935, Autry made regular appearances on top-rated network shows such as *The Lux Radio Theatre* and on the Al Jolson, Eddie Cantor, and Rudy Vallee shows. He also made guest appearances on regional programs like *Listen Ladies* of KEHE in Los Angeles.

In *In Old Santa Fe* Autry appeared in a musical interlude with Smiley Burnette and a band. The setting in *In Old Santa Fe* is a modern-day dude ranch, and Autry and Burnette are the hired entertainment; though the sequence lasts but seven minutes, it incorporates many features that would come to define Autry's later films. Though always signaled as appearing as "himself," his dual presence as both on-screen actor and off-screen musical performer offers some complex plays with audience identification. At the end of the staged performance at the ranch, Autry leaves the bandstand to sing and yodel the film's title song, "In Old Santa Fe." His physical location within the audience, which joins him in the final verse, links Autry symbolically to the crowd, and he performs directly as music star, supposedly unmediated by cinematic construction. Autry's popularity in areas other than film, and his ability to mediate almost seamlessly between his audience and the commercial industries that sought its patronage, explains his success. He was not a skilled actor, but in contrast to the slick professionalism of Hollywood's leading male stars, his halting, almost amateurish, performances further eroded the barriers between him and his constituency. Michele Hilmes, the radio historian, notes: "Hollywood made sure to use the names of its films as part of the titles of its theme songs, so radio—like it or not—would automatically plug its pix when announcing the song titles and recordings played."[13] This was certainly true of the titling of *In Old Santa Fe,* which signals the song and its performance as the film's primary commercial attraction because the picture is set neither in the Old West nor in Santa Fe. It is possible, then, to challenge the orthodox view that radio and records were subordinate media simply fed by film. Rather, the corporate interrelationships and savvy marketing moves suggest a more complex pattern of commercial exchange around Autry that oscillates between cinema, live performance, music recording, and radio productions. For Autry's first starring role in *Tumbling Tumbleweeds* (1935) studio publicity again highlighted his credentials as a radio star. "Radio's Singing Cowboy Takes to the Saddle in a Musical Action-Drama," "The Singing Idol of the Air Now Becomes the Troubadour of the Trail," and "Here's a new screen personality you have heard on the airwaves who now brings to you a new kind of entertainment." Further material in the press book for the film underscores the mutual benefit for exhibitors, record stores, and local music stores if they cross-promote the film and Autry's recording of the title song for Brunswick-Melotone (a subsidiary of Yates's American Record Corporation) as well as a song sheet redesigned by the music publisher M. M. Coles that featured stills from the film.

Though *In Old Santa Fe* was ostensibly a Ken Maynard vehicle, positive exhibitor response identified Autry's performance as its primary attraction. "This is one of the best Westerns I've ever run. I highly recommend it to any fellow exhibitor that uses Westerns. Good story, plenty of thrills, comedy and some good music and singing by Gene Autry and his band. This is the kind of Western that pleases my patrons."[14] This review appeared in *Motion Picture Herald*'s "What the Picture Did for Me," a column of letters that was an important site for independent exhibitors to announce the box-office fortunes of individual titles and to publicize successful promotional events. It also provided space for exhibitors to criticize unfair distribution practices: "The real facts are we play Westerns because they make us money to pay for the clucks we're forced to run, against the better judgment of the wishes of our audience."[15] *In Old Santa Fe* received a number of equally positive recommendations in the pages of the *Motion Picture Herald:* "Why, oh why, doesn't some company produce more Westerns like this one and give us small town exhibitors something to make money on?"[16] "At

last they have learned how to make Westerns. Pulled and pleased
100%. More like this."[17] "No one could ask for a better Western."[18]
"This one holds house record for this year. First musical Western I ever
played."[19] "A good Western with plenty of music and fun. Not the usual shoot 'em up and drag out type, but just a good comical modern
Western. Give us more of this type."[20] "Pleased many who are not Western fans."[21] A year after its release, *In Old Santa Fe* continued to garner
favorable reviews and notices.[22] To sell the film one exhibitor removed
the name of Ken Maynard from his publicity material because he
deemed it a liability: "The success we enjoyed with this picture again
proves the value of the exhibitor's reports. Had it not been for the
glowing tributes paid to this film by fellow exhibitors we would have
relegated this film to our 'B' house and then forgotten about it. However, after reading reports on it we made a radical departure from our
almost set policy of playing everything except Westerns at our A house
and booked it. It took some clever selling and the elimination of Maynard's name from the billing to put it over, but we stood them up and
also received many compliments on the picture."[23] The exhibitor did
not explain how he sold film to an audience that usually shunned
westerns, but the implication is that it was attractive for its musical attributes, as is evident in the following review:

> One of the best bets you can make on Fri-Sat. It's above the average
> and will please not only Western fans, but others more sophisticated.
> The plot is good, it has historical glamor and some really delightful
> Gene Autry music to lift it out of the rut of the common-place shoot-
> ing and fighting which are alright as seasonings but why not make more
> Westerns like this and the O'Brien and Randolph Scott–Zane Grey
> stories? They have general appeal. Most folks (not decadent) like clean
> outdoor adventure, and with a little music and cowboy singing, West-
> erns go over well weekly in my town. And don't you ever think my
> Western fans don't know the difference between these two types of
> Westerns. The box office proves it conclusively.[24]

The references to Autry's musical interlude and to "Zane Grey stories"—in which romance was central—suggest that the western could
reach a broader audience if it incorporated elements that counterbal-
anced the more formulaic episodes of fistfights, shoot-'em-ups, and
chases. As the reviews continued to make apparent, Autry's films were
unprecedented in appealing equally to male and female audiences:
"Gene Autry is fast becoming one of our best box-office attractions, and

our cashier has forgotten Gene Raymond [a minor matinee attraction] in her admiration for Autry."[25] Such inclusive audience appeal is significant in accounting for Autry's box-office success.

The inclusion of musical interludes in western films offered other studios, such as Warner Bros., a route through which to reenter a market that they had abandoned in the early thirties—capitalizing on the established popularity of cowboy music on the radio. The novelty factor is evident in Warner Bros. advertising copy for the studio's series of singing westerns: "'Our hat's in the ring with Westerns that sing.' Dick Foran 'The Singing Cowboy.' Yessir, men, we've got the first new idea in Westerns since Broncho Billy Anderson learned to ride! All the rarin', tearin', ridin' and shootin' of the best of the old time series—plus those *Cowboy Songs* the country's crazy over, featured in every release! That's why you'll have the edge on the other fellow If you'll grab Warner Bros. six Westerns presenting the screen's New-West star Dick Foran. *Moonlight on the Prairie.*"[26] According to the *Motion Picture Herald*'s listings of new films, the Dick Foran vehicle *Moonlight on the Prairie* was ready for distribution on November 2, 1935, while Gene Autry's *Tumbling Tumbleweeds* had a release date of November 9, 1935. The simultaneous release dates suggest that both Warner Bros. and Republic were acting on a common understanding of the appeal of commercial cowboy songs.

Other studios also launched new western series during this season. Columbia promoted a new Charles Starrett series of westerns: "Presenting the first of a new series . . . thrilling romantic adventure stories . . . in Western settings . . . by Peter B. Kyne—millions of men & women—boys and girls—read his famous action yarns. His name is box office!"[27] RKO introduced the novelty of featuring Harry Carey, Hoot Gibson, Guinn "Big Boy" Williams, Bob Steele, and Tom Tyler in *Powder Smoke Range*—"The Barnum & Bailey of Western shows."[28] In advertising copy for its Zane Grey and Hopalong Cassidy series and for a reissue of *The Virginian,* Paramount emphasized its concern for the regional independent exhibitor: "Paramount has not forgotten Sleepy Eye, Minnesota, Smackover, Arkansas, Red Lodge, Montana and 3500 other small towns where folks like red-blooded action in their moving pictures."[29] In early 1936 Paramount further capitalized on the vogue for cowboy songs by starring Bing Crosby in *Rhythm on the Range,* which featured Bing's big hit "I'm an Old Cowhand."[30] That same year MGM located Jeanette MacDonald and Nelson Eddy in a wilderness setting for *Rose Marie* (a.k.a. *Indian Love Call*), while the Poverty Row independent Grand National starred Tex Ritter in *Song of the Gringo.*

Autry came to dominate the new market for singing cowboys. According to the *Motion Picture Herald*'s poll of the top ten western box-office stars, until the arrival of Roy Rogers, Autry's greatest competition came from Tex Ritter, but the competition did not amount to much. In 1936, its first year of polling, Autry came in third, behind Buck Jones, who was first, and and George O'Brien in second place. In 1937 Autry rose to the top of the poll. He would stay there until 1943 when he was deposed by Roy Rogers after Autry had enlisted in the military.[31] Autry's success resulted from how he positioned himself in relation to his audience, particularly in the way he was able to perform that act of integration that suggested he was one of their own.

Warner Bros. failed to generate and maintain a core audience for its singing cowboy, Dick Foran. He collected far fewer recommendations than Autry from exhibitors; Foran's films, at least initially, had good production values and narratives that followed the predictable formula of rescuing a distressed maiden. However, they are set in the historical West and not the contemporary West that Autry inhabits. Foran's songs are overblown compared to Autry's and, though suffused with a bonhomie, lack Autry's intimacy. During the two seasons from 1935 to 1937 Foran made only twelve westerns, most of which locate him within a hermetically sealed fictional universe, whereas Autry's are predicated upon an openness to the contemporary. This is indicated not just in the use of modern-day story settings but more pointedly in narrative structures that actively incorporate popular guest stars from radio. Only the later Foran films featured cameos (as in Autry's films). Foran, alongside other singing cowboys such as Fred Scott, owed more to MGM's operatic matinee idol, Nelson Eddy, than to any tradition of vernacular American music. Warner Bros. may have hoped that Foran would have crossover appeal—playing both to Autry's constituency and to fans of more urbane singers like Eddy and Dick Powell. Powell's 1938 vehicle, *The Cowboy from Brooklyn* (Warner Bros.) parodied the singing cowboy, but, as with Crosby's film *Rhythm of the Range,* exploited the fad for cowboy songs that had been current since Billy Hill's "The Last Roundup" in 1933. However, if that was the case, Warner Bros. would have been disappointed; Foran's westerns made a poor showing across the board. Despite attempts to ape the successful innovations of the Autry film, Foran's series returned only a small profit, averaging about $50,000 per picture, or about $10,000 less than Warner Bros.'s last foray into western production with the John Wayne series of 1932–33, which was released at the depth of the depression.[32]

Soon after his series ended, Foran appeared as a series western cowboy in the James Cagney Hollywood spoof *Boy Meets Girl* (Warner Bros., 1938). The film ruthlessly parodied Foran's character, called the "idol of illiteracy" by Cagney's character. The humor, which depends upon a view of the western's audience as intellectually stunted, measures the patronizing distance of Warner Bros. from the genre's audience, which was much better served by Republic Pictures.

Tex Ritter could never hope to compete effectively with Autry's popularity because meager budgets hamstrung his films. Lindsley Parsons supervised Ritter's films for Grand National, and R. N. Bradbury directed many of them; both had previously worked on John Wayne's Monogram series, and Ritter's films demonstrate all the flaws found there. While, for example, Autry could afford to showcase the talents of Patsy Montana, the first singing cowgirl to sell a million records, the best that Ritter offered in *Arizona Days* was a spot to the harmonica talent of Salty Holmes, a member of Patsy Montana's band, the Prairie Ramblers. Grand National, evidently, could afford neither Patsy Montana nor even the whole of her group. Holmes plays a "fox chase,"

Dick Foran, Warner Bros.'s singing cowpuncher

a fast-paced harmonica showcase complete with animal noises, a performance piece mocked in the Twentieth Century–Fox productions *Pigskin Parade* (1936) and *Tin Pan Alley* (1940).[33] While Ritter had some good original tunes, many of which he composed, he could afford neither the songwriting talents that Autry could draw upon nor the high production values that Autry increasingly used in his recording sessions. Furthermore, Ritter's films did not have the radio exposure that Autry's enjoyed.

Toward the end of 1938 Grand National was in serious financial difficulties, and Ed Finney, Ritter's producer and manager, negotiated a new contract with the recently reformed Monogram. Ritter, however, was far from happy. In a letter to Finney he complained of Monogram's preferential treatment of its other cowboy star, Jack Randall, noting that the company's block bookings were dependent on the popularity of *his* films, not Randall's. Ritter argued that his films deserved an eight-day shooting schedule and at least a $30,000 budget—more than twice the present cost of Monogram's productions. Ritter saved his most withering criticisms for the poor guest acts signed for

Tex Ritter, who presented a rather more hard-boiled exterior than Autry et al.

his films: "Simply glance at the case of the last Autry picture, not one, but four name radio acts, two of the biggest in the business, The Hoosier Hot Shots and The Ranch Boys. Those are the things that put your picture over. For instance the manager at Carrollton, Ky. told me that he couldn't get Rogers started until his third picture when he used Lulu Belle and Scotty of *National Barn Dance* in one of his pictures. Since then he has been one of his four ranking stars."[34]

Ritter made these comments while making a series of personal appearances at cinemas on the southern Wilby-Kincey circuit (Arkansas, Tennessee, Mississippi, Alabama, Kentucky, North Carolina, West Virginia, Washington, D.C., Maryland, Pennsylvania, and Ohio) from July to September 1939. Touring with his band, the Musical Tornadoes (Curly Hogg on electric guitar and banjo, Dick Phillips on electric steel guitar and "ordinary" guitar, and Mike Homer on accordion), Ritter was following a route traveled earlier by the singing cowboys Bob Baker and Roy Rogers. During the same season Ken Maynard, Bob Steele, Ray Corrigan (of the Three Mesquiteers), and Smiley Burnette would also play the circuit. The function of the tours was to promote the western stars' pictures and to provide alternative income during the gaps in the shooting season. An ad in the local paper promoted Ritter's appearance at the Richland Theatre in Carrollton, Kentucky, with an 8-by-10-inch advertisement that noted, "This is the first time that a famous Hollywood star has ever appeared in Carrollton. We know you will be here to welcome him. This is an attraction you cannot afford to miss."[35]

Ritter did good business on the tour, but as *Variety* noted in a short news report, Bob Baker's box office was "way off"; Ray Corrigan "is just getting by, so far as grosses are concerned," and the appeal of Roy Rogers, although he was a "good draw," "lies chiefly with kids."[36] Ritter rarely failed to sell out his evening shows, making on average $150 per day—a considerable amount even after the William Morris Agency (which booked the tour) extracted 10 percent and Ed Finney claimed a further 5. With the remainder Ritter had to cover all his expenses. Nevertheless, he was hardly impoverished, despite his reluctance to reimburse Finney for money owed on his laundry bill. Ritter was playing venues that seated between five hundred and a thousand people, with admission averaging fifteen cents for children and twenty-five cents for adults. Autry, who had also played the southern circuit that season but at only the larger theaters, was clearing more than $1,000 per appearance. *Variety* noted that at the Strand Theatre in Kingsport, Tennessee, "only a 1,000-seater, the theatre grossed $1,200 on the one-day Autry date."[37] By this time Autry was turning down appearances with the *National Barn Dance* at state fairs for which he was offered $1,500 plus traveling expenses.[38] Whether it was record sales, live performances, or films, Autry outdrew all others.

In one of his "tour reports" to Finney, Ritter noted that the lower-than-average box-office earnings at one particular theater had been due to its location in the "poor section" of a small town: "Only two of my pictures had ever played here but the last one drew $80.00 and the average Western business is $55.00 or $60.00. The last Autry picture drew $100.00 for his Saturday record. Reason for this it was published that Autry sing [*sic*] 'It Makes No Difference Now' in the picture. His average Wednesday's business is between $10.00 & $15.00."[39] "It Makes No Difference Now" was a 1938 hit for Jimmie Davis and was featured in the Autry film *Mountain Rhythm* (Republic, 1939). Ritter also featured the song in *Down the Wyoming Trail* (Monogram, 1939). Motivated by comments from his patrons, the manager of the Carolina Theater in South Carolina wrote to the branch manager of the Monogram Southern Exchange to offer the following "constructive criticism of Tex Ritter's pictures":

> The gist of these comments was that they enjoyed hearing Tex sing "It Makes No Difference Now" and wondered why Monogram does not give a personality and a voice like Tex's more old favorites. . . . It is my honest opinion that given songs like "Mexicali Rose," "Down by the Old Mill Stream," "Carolina Moon," "Ride Tenderfoot Ride," "When the Moon Comes Over the Mountain," or any popular numbers both old and new, Tex would really go to town. I believe that the Saturday audiences here much prefer hearing their favorite star sing the old favorites,—no matter how old—to the newer songs with which they are not familiar.[40]

A large number of cinema managers echoed these sentiments about the importance of well-chosen musical material in a report drawn up in 1939 by the Debbs Reynolds Interstate circuit. The circuit distributed "Suggestions to Improve Westerns" to western producers. Here are some typical responses from managers:

> The reaction of the western fan is fundamental and does not change. His desires are for action, action, action, and more action. Secondly, hero worship, and thirdly, comedy. Last, but by no means least, the love of cowboy or mountain music.

Cowboy songs and music has [*sic*] a definite part in western pictures—
it's part of the old west, western patrons like good fiddle bands and
good cowboy songs. I do not mean that the star must sing the songs,
but a band of ranch house boys could all get together and play some
musical numbers and sing a few songs.

The few essentials in making westerns is a good down to earth sensi-
ble story, action, horsemanship, and at present, comedy and some
music.

Westerns have gained a lot by having good music throughout the picture.

Believe that all westerns should have at least two or three good cowboy songs. They don't have to be new ones. Believe the majority enjoy
the old favorite cowboy songs.

The Sons of the Pioneers is the best liked cowboy music in pictures,
but they have not been sold. Tex Ritter has had very little support. Some
of the fans ridicule his singing, but most like it. If he is kept in fast,
snappy songs, he is good, but he is poison in the ballad.

As several managers suggested, the one set of performers that was not
"poison in the ballad" and appears to have been particularly popular
was the Sons of the Pioneers: "The surest way to put over a western
picture is to tie it in with a popular song. The surest way to put over a
series is to tie it in with a popular radio cowboy quartette such as the
Doughboys or the Sons of the Pioneers, or get together a good cowboy quartette or group of singers and sell them. They don't have to
be very good, just sing loud and sing the right songs."[41] Given its base
in Los Angeles and its songwriting talents, the Sons of the Pioneers
quickly found work in the movies, providing the theme songs—"Moonlight on the Prairie" and "Tumbling Tumbleweeds"—for both Dick
Foran's and Gene Autry's first starring vehicles and "Westward Ho" for
John Wayne's first for Republic. In May 1935 the group appeared in a
Vitaphone short, *Radio Scout,* and later made its feature film debut in
The Old Homestead (Liberty, 1935). In the course of that year the Pioneers made seven appearances in shorts and features, including two
outings with Charles Starrett: *Gallant Defender* (Columbia) and *Mysterious Avenger* (Columbia). In 1936 the group made guest appearances
in two Foran movies for Warner Bros., *California Mail* and *Song of the
Saddle.* The Pioneers also appeared in the Autry films *The Big Show* and

The Big Show (1936). Gene Autry at the microphone, Smiley Burnette on Autry's right, and the Sons of the Pioneers to his left. (Photos provided courtesy of the Autry Qualified Interest Trust and the Autry Foundation. © 2001 by the Autry Qualified Interest Trust and the Autry Foundation.)

The Old Corral, both for Republic, and had a cameo spot in Bing Crosby's *Rhythm of the Range* (Paramount). In all these films the camera tends to isolate the best-looking member of the group, Roy Rogers (Len Slye, as he was then called), while the others appear dull and ill at ease in front of the camera.

In 1937 Rogers separated from the Pioneers and under a new name—Dick Weston—appeared in the Three Mesquiteers' *Wild Horse Rodeo* (Republic) and Autry's *The Old Barn Dance.* By late 1937 Slye was releasing solo records under the name of Roy Rogers. Republic put him under contract to star in *Under Western Stars,* which was released in the spring of 1938. The film had originally been planned as an Autry vehicle titled *Washington Cowboy,* but the star had walked out on the studio after executives refused to renegotiate his contract. Autry's demands were motivated by the knowledge that Republic's block-booking policy was dependent on the popularity of his films. That is, to secure the new series of Autry westerns an exhibitor also had to book the rest of Republic's productions. According to the western film historian Karl Thiede, Mascot had originally hired Autry at $75 a week. With the move to Republic Pictures, his wages increased to $100, with raises of $50 a week for every six months that he remained at the studio. A new contract drawn up in 1936 gave Autry $2,000 per picture (eight per season), and Republic doubled that amount the following year. By 1938 Republic was paying him $5,000 per picture, but Autry wanted $15,000.[42] A contemporary news item in the *New York Times* claimed the studio was offering $10,000, but Autry (the paper misspelled his name as "Autrey") was demanding $25,000.[43]

While on "strike" Autry filled his time and maintained his bank balance by touring. The news item suggests that Autry could earn the equivalent of two years' salary from Republic by undertaking a five-month tour of South America. In other words, he did not need Republic as much as it needed him. Autry soon made a deal with Republic that, according to the film historian Douglas Gomery, increased his salary by nearly 1,000 percent; he also won an increase in his films' budgets. The studio history *Republic Confidential* records that the new contract offered $6,000 for each of the first two pictures that he completed and $10,000 for each film for the remainder of the season. This then rose to $11,000 per picture for the 1940–41 season, $12,000 for 1941–42, and $13,000 for 1942–43. In 1936–37 his films cost $50,000 to $75,000 to produce and grossed more than $500,000.[44] However, the immediate effect of Autry's absence was to give an early opportunity to Roy Rogers to prove his box-office potential.

Though Rogers gave a solid performance in *Under Western Stars,* he lacked the familiarity of Autry that bound the older star so firmly to the community that he represented. Rogers sings six songs in the film, one of which allows him to display his particular talents for yodeling, while another allows him to assume the role of a square dance caller (an act he had developed before he joined the Pioneers). But other than that, he has no established and distinctive persona to draw upon. In the films that immediately followed, Rogers's singing interludes would be cut back to an average of two or three per picture (Autry's films under his new contract would increase his number of songs). Paring the musical content was an attempt by Republic to differentiate the Autry and Rogers films. The trade magazine *Exhibitor* noted as much when it reported: "Republic decided Autry should be its singing buckaroo, that Rogers should be its action caballero, and that the

Roy Rogers

Three Mesquiteers should be its general purpose trio. Thus there would be no over-lapping of functions, and the three series would be separate and distinct."[45]

Unlike Autry's films, Rogers's tended to be set in the past. They featured historical characters such as Billy the Kid, Jesse James, Buffalo Bill, and Bill Hickok or used historical time periods, such as the end of the Spanish-American War, the Civil War, and the Pony Express era.

The final act of differentiation was that the time, effort, and money supplied for Autry's films were not spent on Rogers's.

Nevertheless, the evidence of the films themselves suggests that Republic was convinced it had an actor in Roy Rogers rather than, as with Autry, a singing phenomenon. Rogers's vehicles are much more carefully plotted and provide dramatic situations not found in Autry films. In *Arizona Kid* (Republic, 1939) Rogers plays the part of a young Missourian just returned from Arizona. After the outbreak of the Civil War, he joins the regular Confederate Army rather than a band of guerrillas that loots and terrorizes the local civilian population. When Roy finally catches up with the gang, he holds a field court marshal and condemns the band to death by firing squad. Among those who will die is his childhood friend. Within the logic of the film Roy's actions are entirely justified; he had given his friend a number of chances to quit the marauders. But the film poses a moral dilemma that is extremely rare in series westerns. The following year Rogers would have a supporting role in Republic's *The Dark Command,* which represented the studio's second attempt (after the 1939 *Man of Conquest*) at producing a picture designed for first-run theaters.

Rogers sings two songs in *Arizona Kid.* The first is the spiritual "Swing Low, Sweet Chariot," where he joins in with a black singing group. "Who's dat singing like an angel?" says Mammy Lou, tacitly authenticating the star's performance. "It's Master Roy, himself," replies another black servant slave. The second is the blackface minstrel number "Lazy Old Moon." In *Frontier Pony Express* (Republic, 1939), Rogers sings the Stephen Foster composition "My Old Kentucky Home." The two films' Civil War setting partly sanctioned use of these antebellum minstrel tunes, but Rogers had specialized in such popular songs as a member of the Sons of the Pioneers. The choice of musical material was a further attempt to differentiate him from Autry.

Exhibitors' reports in the *Motion Picture Herald* were, on the whole, fairly positive toward Rogers's pictures: "Advertised Lulu Belle and Scotty in a long way and drew in some extra business, but this Western [*Shine on Harvest Moon*] was good enough and this boy Rogers is doing all right with us."[46] "This boy is getting better and with Smiley Burnette and his music to help, he can't miss. There is plenty of action and a lot of singing and music and that seems to be what my patrons crave."[47] "This kid has taken Autry's place as the number one box office Western star. Autry just does average Sat. business but Rogers does about 20 percent above average."[48] But along with the last commentary remarking on on Autry's apparently fading box-office popularity, another contributor to that edition's "What the Picture Did for Me" wrote: "There is a Santa Claus and I don't mean maybe. Played this [*The Old Barn Dance*] with [a] Laurel and Hardy comedy and they came in droves. Gene, I want to thank you from the bottom of my heart for the merriest Christmas I ever had, and look forward to playing every one of your pictures in 1939. Brother exhibitors play this one."

Until Autry joined the armed forces, his popularity remained unchallenged. Rogers made his reputation in the years after 1943 when he teamed up with Dale Evans, who allowed his films to focus in a novel manner on domestic intrigue. Foran, Scott, Jack Randall (Monogram, 1937–38), Smith Ballew (Twentieth Century–Fox, 1937–38), and Bob Baker (Universal, 1937–40) had little staying power. For the most part they appeared as they were—actors playing a role. With an already established persona and a large and loyal radio audience, Autry deepened and further cemented his relationship with his growing constituency, particularly with the women in his audience.

The publicity releases by Republic reveal an overriding concern with producing films that will appeal not just to men or women but to the whole family. The initial effort is to highlight a film's appeal for children: "Take a look at all the things Gene doesn't do in *Rootin' Tootin' Rhythm*. To begin with, he doesn't do anything which would offend the army of small boys who worship him, or put bad ideas into their heads." However, as the p.r. story develops, this emphasis on clean living and wholesomeness clearly is principally addressed to mothers: "Coins for theatre tickets come from Mama's purse, and Mama isn't going to send her young hopeful to see a screen hero who smokes, drinks, and uses bad or rough language." In fact, "Mama" will probably be sitting alongside Junior and the other members of her family. A common exhibitor ploy was to advertise a free ticket or some other giveaway for any child who was accompanied by three adults—thereby bringing in the extended family.

Although there does not appear to be any material evidence of the precise composition of the audience for series westerns, partial records of Tex Ritter's 1939 personal appearance tour have survived and provide clues. Despite the many publicity images of Tex outside theaters and surrounded by young admirers, and contemporary commentary that cites them as the major consumers of westerns, children did not make up the majority of the audience for Ritter's personal appearances. Box-office receipts show that adults at evening performances outnumbered children on average by 3 to 1 and on some occasions by as much as 4 or 5 to 1. At weekday matinee shows adults outnumbered kids on average by 2 to 1. Given that these daytime weekday shows were unlikely to draw working men, most of the adults must have been female—only for Saturday matinees do children outnumber adults.[49]

Little of the twelve thousand pieces of fan mail that Autry is said to have received each week by the end of the 1930s has survived. However, a few letters penned by Grace Dugan, who proclaimed herself "Public Autry Fan #1," provide further clues to the nature of Autry's female fan base. These date from 1937 to 1941 and reveal one fan's attempts to document her obsession. Beautifully illustrated and designed, and written with a quiet passion for her idol, each letter offers constructive criticism of Autry's latest picture or record release and keeps him in touch with her progress at school (she was seventeen in 1939). She maintained a large circle of pen pals—all women—and would edit and paste up their comments, which she then sent to Autry as a postscript to her own commentary. Many letters record her long-standing and tireless correspondence with fan magazines and newspapers as she worked at her role as self-appointed public relations manager for Autry. One such letter, printed in the *Milwaukee Journal*, engendered a small rash of responses that she cut and pasted and sent to Autry. Commenting on her own letter, she wrote, "I started it with this weepy eulogy (what a style of writing I'm developing! Long, dreary sentences bogged down with adjectives!)." On the first response she wrote, "And then some grumpy old prune wrote this stupid drivel." The "prune" was a Larry F. Daniels, who had the audacity to write that the "monotonous whining of his is certainly the lowest form of singing, if it can qualify as singing at all." Daniels also questioned why it was that "none of the big movie theatres show his pictures if he is so popular?" The respondents to his letter—three women and a man—were unanimous in their support of Autry, though beyond a love for his music they stressed different aspects of his appeal. The male correspondent emphasized the issue of class: "The reason why not many large theatres show Autry's pictures is because they aren't high class enough for the 'high-falutin' class of people," while the women focus on his "sex appeal." Grace Dugan had praised Autry at the expense of other male stars whom she characterized as "parlor sharks," suggesting that Autry's apparent lack of overt sexuality was a positive aspect of his appeal. Mabel Shope responded to the "prune" comment by saying that "Gene Autry is one of the best cowboy singers we have ever had and also a very good actor; the fact that he is a little bashful makes it a little better yet."[50] In the terminology of the day Autry had sex appeal—this is repeated throughout Grace Dugan's letters by both she and her army of pen pals, but it was a sex appeal that was neither threatening nor overtly physical. To his young female fans Autry offered a reassuring image of fantasized romantic involvement that transcended the desires of the body.

In a 1935 article on "horse operas" the *New York Times* attempted to delineate the series western story formula: "The true Western follows strict lines," reports the writer before outlining what he considers to be the form's salient details. The hero, after returning home, finds his father or pal killed and sets out to avenge their deaths. In the pursuit of justice, and by sheer physical effort, he overcomes all obstacles placed in his path. These conflicts are provided by "fights over irrigation rights, railroad rights of way, dams and mines": "Little time is spent in establishing characterization. The plot gets started and, as soon as possible, gets violent. Such things as innuendoes, psychological problems and anti-climaxes worry not the producer of the Western. Hate is hate, love is love and the shooting must start quickly. The hero must conduct himself in a high-class, A1 manner and must not gamble, smoke or drink."[51] The Manichaean world of the western that this writer describes is set forth for a readership that has little knowledge and probably little regard for the form. The emphasis on the western's rejection of characterization, innuendo, and psychological problems separates the "horse opera" from middle-class drama.

The mocking tone of the article confirms the lower status afforded this type of entertainment, yet despite the writer's rather glib attitude and base generalizations, he is essentially correct in his observations. Applying to the series western critical tools drawn from the study of literature and legitimate drama has little value, because all they will reveal are the form's weaknesses, inadequacies, and simplifications. The critical focus, then, should not be on the filmmakers' creation of an illusion of reality, nor upon the form's narrative structure, nor upon characterization—the key areas for determining the value of more "legitimate" dramatic forms. The makers of, and audiences for, series westerns clearly gave little consideration to these areas. Their focus was upon the acts of performance: horse chases, fistfights, courtship, slapstick comedy, and, what was most important in singing westerns, the music. Rather than understand performance as an act of illusion where the trick is to convince viewers that they are not watching actors, the series western celebrated performance as an act of value in and of itself.

FIVE

Cowboy Minstrels: Series Westerns and Musical Performance

Have you by chance a rollicking cowboy roundelay in your repertoire?
  —*Knight of the Plains* (1939)

Other western stars, not least Ken Maynard, had featured musical performances in their films before Gene Autry did. In a promotional photograph released in 1930, Maynard is posed playing the fiddle. If not for his reputation as a screen cowboy, he could be mistaken for one of the many recording and radio cowboys. Indeed, his recording of "The Lone Star Trail," released by Columbia to coincide with the Universal picture *The Wagon Master* (1930), is the only appearance by a "singing cowboy" on Harry Smith's important collection of commercially recorded prewar "folk music," *Anthology of American Folk Music* (1952). The original release billed Maynard as "The American Boy's Favorite Cowboy," but for Smith, Maynard's "passionate" rendition of the song constitutes one of the "very few recordings of authentic cowboy life."[1] This is a curious accolade, given Maynard's career as a film cowboy. But listening to "The Lone Star Trail," or any of the other seven songs that Maynard recorded at the same session, makes clear why he finds a comfortable home on the anthology alongside the likes of

Charlie Patton, Mississippi John Hurt, Frank Hutchison, and the Carter Family. In an essay about Smith's anthology the music critic Greil Marcus notes: "[Maynard] ambles out of the soundtrack of *The Wagon Master* to chant and moan, yodel and wail, stare and tremble, more alone, more stoic and more restless between heaven and nature, than anyone has been before. The shape of the land, its vast expanse, its indifference to who you are or what you want, looms up as this solitary figure says his piece: I am the first cowboy and the last. Here no one sees me, myself least of all, I am happy, I am free."[2] Maynard's thin voice may for some listeners reflect untutored authenticity, but, putting poetic license aside and removing him from the rich tapestry of the anthology, a more prosaic assessment is that he was a rotten singer. Though he continued to feature cowboy songs in his movies, notably in *The Strawberry Roan* (1933) and *Fiddlin' Buckaroo* (1933), he did not continue to make records.

The performances of both Autry and his sidekick, Smiley Burnette, depart from the musical interludes of earlier westerns and propose a distinct mutation in their filmic incorporation. Rather than integrating musical performance seamlessly—as spontaneous singalong around the campfire, as unobserved and private moment, or as serenade to a sweetheart on a ranch house porch—Autry's films frame it explicitly as musical performance. My point is that there is a marked difference between westerns in which cowboys sing and the singing western proper, which rests upon a highly distinctive reflexivity in the representation of musical performance. Unlike Marcus's romantic version of the cowboy as an alienated artist, musical performance in singing westerns is a commonplace act that calls attention to the social bond between the entertainer and his audience. The singing cowboy comes from and speaks to a commonality; he is in partnership with, rather than set apart from, his audience. The strategies that Autry's films use to secure this contract are diverse: trading on the public performance opportunities of the traveling show or barn dance; dismantling the distance between professional music artist and amateur film character in the "spontaneous" performance in bunkhouse or parlor; and using recording/radio technologies as narrative conceits that collapse, rather than uphold, audience distinctions between film character, radio performer, and recording artist.

In *Tumbling Tumbleweeds* and *Guns and Guitars* (Republic, 1936), Autry is the star attraction of Dr. Parker's Phamous Purveyors of Phun Phrolic & Painless Panaceas medicine show. Autry wears his familiar flamboyant costumes of tailored cowboy suits: light-colored, neatly creased shirts and pants with piping around the pockets. The tight-fitting pants are tucked into highly decorated boots, and he wears a neckerchief and Stetson—of the kind that B. M. Bower describes as the "musical comedy brand." Autry, then, appears not as a proletarian cowpuncher but as a musical performer—he is, after all, playing himself. The film emphasizes his sartorial distinctiveness in order to contrast him with both the working cowhands and the evidently proletarian townspeople dressed in contemporary 1930s workwear. Yet, despite differences in apparel (which in any case are warranted by his occupation as a showman), Autry nonetheless functions as a representative of these working-class communities. In *Tumbling Tumbleweeds* he sides with the homesteaders against his rancher father, and, though initially a stranger to the community, toward the end of *Guns and Guitars* he is an elected representative. While both films overtly narrate stories that install Autry as community representative, the musical performances within them truly establish, demonstrate, and secure his democratic credentials. These films partly achieve the blurring of the boundaries between performer and audience through the use of the medicine show as a platform for Autry's public performances. In the context of the 1930s the medicine show was an anachronism, superseded by radio and particularly the semilegitimate stations that broadcast from Mexico. The films use the nostalgic symbol of the medicine show to link Autry, best known through the contemporary media of radio and recordings, to more traditional forms of entertainment. Publicity material for *Rootin' Tootin' Rhythm* (Republic, 1937) used Autry's own brief experience of playing with the Fields Brothers Medicine Show in precisely this manner: "It was a carefree existence, vagabonding from one town to another, with Gene playing his guitar and crooning western songs while the Fields brothers sold nostrums for every human ache and pain. 'The side of our wagon would let down, forming a sort of stage,' Gene reminisces. 'There the barker would stand, luring prospective customers with our hearty if not quite polished stage performances. I was only fourteen at the time, and my father soon yanked me back to the parental fold, but it was paradise while it lasted.'"[3] The studio had used this publicity angle before, in the promotional material for *Tumbling Tumbleweeds* ("a story of an old-time medicine show"). Significantly, the press book records Autry's boyhood reminiscence as recalling an anonymous "travelling cowboy medicine show".[4] Both examples of film publicity patently use such retrospective gloss to reinvent the medicine show as an unadulterated "cowboy" entertainment vehicle. What this does is efface its actual history within the performance traditions of blackface minstrelsy by substituting cowboy songs for minstrel tunes and cowboy performers for blackface entertainers.[5] As the publicity for *Tumbling Tumbleweeds* delineates, "The use of this background enables the famous songwriter [Autry] to present many of his newest numbers and also his biggest selling favorite 'Silver Haired Daddy of Mine.'" Indeed, the recording is played on a phonograph during a medicine show performance in the film, and copies are offered free with every bottle of elixir sold.

Though Republic's publicity office reinvented the medicine show as a form of cowboy entertainment, both *Tumbling Tumbleweeds* and *Guns and Guitars* represent the show's true heritage in minstrelsy by featuring the tap-dancing character played by the African-American Eugene Jackson. Given the racially derogatory name Eightball, costumed in an "Uncle Sam" outfit (satin stovepipe pants, tails, waistcoat, and top hat), and performing in a style that ties him conclusively to blackface entertainment, the character is the embodiment of the tradition of minstrelsy. However, he is also mute throughout both films, which suggests limits to the meaning of the figure's presence. In other words, the minstrel figure appears and thus attests to historical authenticity yet is invoked as silence, a submerged figure without voice. The films' evocation of minstrels and cowboys posits a circulation of meaning that transforms relations between the old and the new, the traditional and the invented; just as old-time music presents itself as both anachronistic *and* contemporary, the musical performances' play with history and the present demarcates the larger domain of the singing western.

In *Oh, Susanna!* Autry is again in the company of traveling minstrels. The troupe (made up of Autry, Burnette, and Earl Hodgins, who perform alongside the Light Crust Doughboys) has signed up to entertain at a dude ranch for vacationing urban middle classes. Repeating the performance setting of *In Old Santa Fe,* the troupe entertains an audience of dudes dressed flamboyantly in "Hollywood western" attire. The Doughboys begin the evening's entertainment with a medley of "Oh, Susanna!" and "Tiger Rag," while Autry turns tricks with a lariat. At the medley's end the Doughboys segue into "He Never Came Through with the Ring," and Professor Deacon Daniels (Hodgins), dressed as a nineteenth-century German college boy, and Frog Millhouse (Burnette's character in Autry films), dressed in the clothes of an old spinster, enter singing the song while riding on an antique bicycle built for two. The scene mixes new and old performance traditions—Frog's drag act and his duet with the professor draw upon nineteenth-century vaudeville. Frog and the professor's comic rendition of "He Never Came Through with the Ring" parodies turn-of-the-century sentimental ballads such as "Those Wedding Bells Shall Not Ring Out," "Take Back Your Gold," and "She May Have Seen Better Days." This is set alongside the western swing of the Light Crust Doughboys, who jazz up Stephen Foster's old minstrel number and turn the jazz standard "Tiger Rag" (a song first recorded by the Original Dixieland Jazz Band) into a country breakdown. Meanwhile, Autry dances with a lasso (a skill that Will Rogers popularized earlier during his stint with the *Ziegfeld Follies*) and sings a sweet serenade to a young woman. This short interlude offers a compact variety bill of entertainment: sophisticated and down-home, traditional and modern, mediated and unmediated, comic and sentimental, active and romantic. In playing to the audience of middle-class dudes, the film suggests that Autry's appeal transcends class boundaries, even when earlier in this film his "natural" constituency had been represented by working men and women who listen to his radio shows and buy his records.

In both *Tumbling Tumbleweeds* and *Guns and Guitars* Autry makes his particular claim to be the community's representative through the establishment of his unimpeachable honesty. The process of confirming Autry's credentials as trustworthy and sincere is particularly pronounced in those films that use Autry's persona as a radio star. Both *Mexicali Rose* (Republic, 1939) and *The Old Barn Dance* (Republic, 1938) meditate the potential consequences for Autry's audience of his ethical detachment from them. Autry twice plays a character who is at first unaware that someone is exploiting his good name for criminal ends. In *Mexicali Rose* he plays a radio star on a Texas-Mexico border station; the sponsor of the program is an oil company that uses Autry's popularity to sell stock that turns out to be worthless. In *The Old Barn Dance* Autry is a horse dealer who uses a barn dance to promote the sale of his animals. Unbeknown to Autry, the shows are being broadcast on a radio show sponsored by a crooked finance company that has been providing loans for farmers to buy tractors. The finance company forecloses on the farmers when they are unable to meet their debts—thus securing title to their land. Both the selling of fraudulent stock and the difficulties in making repayments on bank loans are obvious depression motifs. Autry's role on the radio initially implicates him in the nefarious schemes of the villains but, after he learns of his unwitting involvement, the drive of the narrative is to clear his name and make good the damage done to the community.

As unwitting accomplice brought to action, Autry enacts a narrative of ethical restitution that reconfirms the public's trust in radio and in Autry as agent of community values. The process of mediation between the musician and his audience involves what Robert Cantwell suggests is a complex act of "mimesis." Cantwell writes that mimesis "emphasizes the voluntary reintegration of the mediating figure with the human order which he has transcended but in which his whole nature and character is rooted and to which, therefore, he must periodically return symbolically."[6] As a professional entertainer, Autry is set apart from his audience but, through the kinds of narrative conceits seen in films such as *The Old Barn Dance*, "symbolically" reconfirms the bond with his constituency. In these films the money and fame that he receives as an entertainer have not separated Autry from his rural hometown—he still shares the community's core values and beliefs. As such, Autry aids the citizens in their hour of difficulty because he is one of them, but, unlike the townspeople, ranchers, and farmers, his cowboy and star persona grants him the ability to transcend the mundane. He is a professional entertainer *and* a worker among workers. *The Old Barn Dance* neatly conflates the two dimensions. Ostensibly, Autry stages the barn dance show to sell horses, and Autry sings only to attract customers, yet for Autry business is but a platform that allows him the pleasure of singing. The "naturalness" of this collapse between work and leisure distances Autry from the sense that he is exploiting his audience as potential customers. However, the show is surreptitiously broadcast on radio, compromising the supposedly unmediated pleasure of singing for "the folk." This transforms the performance into a mediated event that, in this context, opens it up to exploitation by the very finance company that has dispossessed Autry's community. By falsely claiming to be the show's sponsor in order to expropriate Autry's good standing, the company's subversion of Autry's "honest" performance engenders a narrative whose real task is to rescue and restore Autry's authenticity as a radio star *and* man of the people. Thus he is a performer created through radio yet unaffected and apparently unaware of his mediated status.

This legitimates Autry's mediation between capital and labor that occurs throughout his film work during the 1930s. Autry is constructed as outside capitalist exploitation, a site of benign consumption. The film's presentation of the various transactions between supposedly unmediated communal get-togethers and their expropriation by corporate interests is complex. On one hand, Autry is recruited to an ideological operation that safeguards the "rural community" from exploitation and testifies to the valence of images of the countryside uncontaminated by the encroachments of modernity and consumption. On the other, such disavowal of capitalist interest effaces Autry's location within the very commodity structures that regulate his place in commercial exchange. Through radio, advertising, and record production, Autry's music is as inescapably tied to commodity culture as to community performance. Such doubling is echoed in the representation of the community and its workaday rituals, which are thus transformed into a commercial cinematic spectacle for the audiences of Republic Pictures, Incorporated.

Time and again within his films the audiences for Autry's public musical performances are farmers and other rural workers, who were also considered to be the primary consumers of his films, records, and radio programs. Though these communities undoubtedly formed a core constituency, Autry also had a large urban following, and many of these fans would have been first-generation migrants from the rural South and Midwest. The invoking of a rural community threatened by mechanization would still have profound meaning for these newly urban industrial laborers. For his urban audience Autry's eventual filmic reintegration into the community was not just an act of mimesis on his part but also symbolized a connection to their recent past. Similarly, the medicine shows in *Tumbling Tumbleweeds* and *Guns and Guitars* and the barn dance in *The Old Barn Dance* function as symbolic connections to a shared agrarian history. The performance sites and rituals suggest a tradition outside history, a form of entertainment that remains uncorrupted by the modern media but is in fact a product of the new media technologies. Just as the minstrel and the cowboy in Autry's medicine shows represented the old and the new, the barn dance draws upon the idea of a rural communal get-together but is a modern innovation. The variety format presented in the films belonged wholly to a commercialized system of entertainment.

The use of semipublic spaces, such as the sheriff's office and jailhouse, enables a range of performances that are both public and private. In *The Old Corral* (Republic, 1936) the jailhouse is the site for a one-man-band piece by Smiley and two spots by the film's guest stars, the Sons of the Pioneers. Just before the film ends, it is also where a phonograph plays a recording of the title song; Gene and the female lead are superimposed over the image of the phonograph, which fades out on their kiss. The film does not bother with a narrative justification for the playing of a Gene Autry record (though its presence has the commercial motivation of promoting Autry's recording), but it does, along with the formation of the couple, symbolize the domestication of the jailhouse. This in turn signals an end to the various criminal shenanigans that have so evidently destabilized the community. *Oh, Susanna!* features Autry's phonograph recordings on three occasions, each with at least some narrative justification. First, Autry is mistaken for a killer and is imprisoned; to prove he is Gene Autry he has to sing before a group of his radio fans, who have been invited to the jailhouse. Unfortunately, for Gene his voice was damaged earlier in a fight. Saving the day, Smiley steals a phonograph and an Autry record that some old-timers on a street corner were listening to and secretly plays it under the jailhouse window. Gene lip-synchs and convinces the audience of his "true" identity. Meanwhile, the killer for whom Autry was mistaken has assumed his identity and calls upon a family that runs a dude ranch; the phony Autry arrives as the family members are gathered around their phonograph, listening to another Autry recording that seemingly confirms the killer's masquerade. The third use of a recording occurs once more at the dude ranch, again to substantiate Autry's identity, this time by the villains, who lip-synch to a phonograph recording of Autry. The combined effect of these instances of tying Autry's identity to phonograph recordings is to authenticate both the entertainer and his products. The authentication of the performer and his material is essential in order to shore up the multiplicity of identities that he presents to his audience. As "Gene Autry," he is a singer in front of live audiences, on radio, on records, and he is an actor, as well as a performer of rodeo tricks. He is also a sponsored entertainer, that is to say, an advertiser. This is promotion on a grand scale. The film acts to unite the multiple performances, personas, and audiences by means of Autry's appearance on screen before the cinema spectators.

Autry's films use less contested spaces for musical and other forms of divertissement, in particular the domesticated and seemingly amateur forms of entertainment practiced in bunkhouses and parlors. Following an expository montage under the opening credits for *Rootin' Tootin' Rhythm,* the film begins in the parlor of Autry's ranch house where various cowboys and their kinfolk are gathered. Gene is lead-

ing them in the singing of "I Hate to Say Goodbye to the Prairie," and
as the song progresses, individuals (including an obese young boy in
a cowboy outfit) take solo spots before the song is taken up by a cowboy riding night herd. The film returns to the parlor, the song ends,
and a band of cowpunchers arrives looking for work. A display of ea-
gle-eyed shooting of whiskey glasses confirms their credentials, but the
real test is when they have to sing along with first Smiley and then Gene.
They do just fine. The cowboys are in fact Al Clauser and his Oklahoma Outlaws, a western swing outfit that had an immensely popular
show broadcast from Des Moines that by 1938 was carried by 272
Mutual network stations.[7] Though the cowboys in the gang are not who
they first appear to be (they are rangers on the trail of rustlers), only
the film's credits reveal their real-life identity. Yet in this sequence and
a later one in a bunkhouse, their musical ability stalls the action and
holds every other character at rapt attention. Many of Autry's serenades
to the leading female function in a similar manner. In *Guns and Guitars* the action stops while he sings "Dreamy Valley." At first, it is not
certain to whom, if anyone, the performance is directed. The film
shows Autry in profile and close-up; as the song progresses, the camera moves down to the guitar and pauses on the neck, where the name
Gene Autry is inlaid in pearl. The camera then continues in the same
direction, eventually revealing the presence of the film's romantic lead
(Dorothy Dix), who is utterly captivated by his performance. She is a
surrogate for members of the cinema audience, held, we can surmise,
in an equally enchanted trance by Autry's singing and his "sex appeal,"
as defined by Grace Dugan and her army of pen pals. When the song
finishes, the spell is broken, and Autry, like the medicine show, is on
the move again, staying just long enough to once again forge a bond
with the community (and to sell his records, his sponsor's goods, and
the products he endorses). "Tamed characters do have our confidence," writes W. T. Lhamon Jr., "but not our memory. They are not
legendary."[8] By offering himself as both static and in motion, Autry
gains his audience's confidence and its awe. This was not always the
case for Autry's competitors.

 The Devil's Saddle Legion (Warner Bros., 1937)—the demonic promise of the title is not fulfilled—introduces Dick Foran, riding, singing,
and yodeling. His carefree attitude quickly disappears when he is accused of murder and then sentenced to work as part of a prison gang.
This scenario does not present him as a professional entertainer, but
he nevertheless sings to his cell mates and to the daughter of a ranch-

er. The big musical number performed alongside a river matches these semipublic performances. Tilting his head toward the sky, Foran sings of his "prairie home" (he locates himself here in at least one song per film), which is also "God's country," "the Master's ranch on earth," where "even trees reach up in prayer." This little slice of operetta is markedly at odds with Autry's style—it is a virtuoso's showcase. It does not link Foran to an audience; rather, it separates him and emphasizes his uniqueness. The performance and song owe little to the tradition in which Autry worked.

Fred Scott was another actor and singer who had a middlebrow musical training similar to Foran's. Both were big men with stomachs that sat uneasily over their belts, their podgy physiognomy giving them a juvenile and guileless appearance. Scott had the added attraction of a toothy grin so luminous that it would be the last image remaining on the screen after it had faded to black. The Poverty Row studio Spectrum Pictures signed Scott in 1936, and he would star in almost two dozen cowboy pictures. His films shifted between historical and con-

The ever-smiling Fred Scott, in a scene from *In Old Montana* (1939)

temporary settings, and in some he would appear as a cowboy who liked to break into song, while in others he would appear as an entertainer.

In his 1939 release, *In Old Montana*, Scott plays a cavalry officer who works undercover as a singer in a medicine show in order to bring peace between the cattlemen and the sheepherders. The first musical number is a comedy song, "Get Along Mule," in which he performs a yodeling duet with his sidekick. The yodel is in the Tyrolean tradition, an elaborate and virtuoso vocal demonstration, a yodeling frippery in which Autry did not indulge. Scott's next number comes after a chase that ends with his being pulled from his horse after getting caught in a wash line. To make amends he helps the heroine with her chores. With arms covered in soap suds he sings of the pleasure gained "from washing clothes all day" and being a "mother's helper." As in other films, such as in *Knight of the Plains* (Spectrum, 1939), where he sings "Home Sweet Home" accompanied on a pedal organ by an elderly lady in her parlor, the wash scene displays the domestic and sentimental sides of the singing cowboy. This is the dramatic equivalent of the mawkishness of turn-of-the-century and vernacular "Mother" songs. As with Foran, Scott's trained, accentless voice has the effect of distancing the performer from the vernacular tradition upon which Autry maintained a hold. However, the domestic scenarios in Scott's westerns effectively perform a similar function of maintaining the singing cowboy's link to the community through "home"—be it ever so humble.

Tex Ritter had a keener understanding of the cowboy song tradition. Before his 1930 move to New York, where he secured work for the 1930–31 season in the Broadway production of *Green Grow the Lilacs* (later turned into the Rodgers and Hammerstein musical *Oklahoma!*), Ritter studied at the University of Texas at Austin. As a member of the glee club, he came under the influence of the Texas folklorist J. Frank Dobie and the voice tutor Oscar J. Fox. With a song bag filled with cowboy songs drawn from Lomax's and Dobie's collections, Ritter bypassed the Jimmie Rodgers influence that held so many of his peers in thrall and presented himself instead as a cowboy singer. Following his stint on Broadway, Ritter worked in radio and recorded for American Record Corporation and then for Decca.[9] Though he recorded covers of hit songs such as Jimmie Davis's "Nobody's Darling but Mine" (1935), most of Ritter's records were fairly straight interpretations of cowboy songs drawn from published collections. He did not yodel, and he sang in a lower register than most of his contemporary vernacular singers. Ritter took this artful authenticity with him when he moved to California in 1936 to star in a series of singing westerns that the recently formed Grand National planned in the wake of Autry's success.[10]

Ritter's films featured both established cowboy songs and new compositions. *Arizona Days* (Grand National, 1937) introduces him in typical singing cowboy style, riding and singing alongside his sidekick. The chosen song is "Tombstone, Arizona," a new composition and worth quoting:

> I'm a howling fool from Texas
> With a six-gun in my sack,
> I eat rattlesnakes for breakfast
> My coffin's on my back.
> I've got a bobcat for a partner
> And we get along just fine,
> I sharpen my teeth on tombstones
> Just to pass the time.

In stark contrast to Foran's heavenly odes, this imagery reaches back to the early nineteenth-century ring-tailed roarer tales of the Davy Crockett almanacs. It was also expressed in contemporary blues songs such as Lonnie Johnson's "Got the Blues for Murder Only" (1930)—"Women down in Old Mexico, as bad as bad can be. / They eats rattlesnakes for breakfast and drinks the rattlesnake's blood for tea"—and the later Bo Diddley's "Who Do You Love?" (1956)—"I walk forty-seven miles of barbed wire, / I use a cobra snake for a necktie."[11] Autry would leave the bragging comic numbers for Smiley Burnette; Ritter's sidekick in *Arizona Days* cannot play the trombone that he carries through much of the film, nor does he sing, so the star plays and sings the comic, romantic, and stirring numbers.

Like Autry's, Ritter's films often characterize him as a professional musician or as an aspiring musician, as in *Arizona Days* where he joins an impoverished traveling troupe (Professor McGill's Minstrel Show: The Biggest Little Show in the West). On opening night Ritter sings "High, Wide, and Handsome," and, as in Autry's films, the small-town audience is composed of rural workers—only the villains and Ritter wear cowboy apparel. Ritter did not dress in the elaborate western stage costumes that Tom Mix first displayed and that Autry preferred. Instead, Ritter sports a more proletarian look, wearing blue jeans with a six-inch turn-ups (rather small compared to Bing Crosby's in *Rhythm of the Range*, which reach almost to his knee), plain shirts, and suede

Crockett thumbs his nose at authority and rides his pet alligator up
Niagara Falls

jackets worn shiny on the arms and front. Foran tended to wear black western costumes that contrasted with the grays of the supporting cast. Ritter, though, dresses up a little for his debut performance in *Arizona Days*—a new white hat and a decorated calfskin waistcoat.

As a cowboy, Ritter is differentiated from his audience, but the functionality of his costume locates him within the same class status. A scene from *Sing Cowboy Sing* (Grand National, 1937) exemplifies his ability to address his audience in an apparently unmediated fashion akin to Autry's. Ritter and his partner are locked up in jail on trumped-up charges, but rather than let this get him down, Ritter proposes to sing his way out of the blues and, metaphorically, out of jail. Turning to the camera, he looks directly into the lens, introduces his song, and then sings it—effectively violating the camera's supposed invisibility. Responding to the question of which actors had an influence on his work, Tex Ritter once said, "I have been influenced by none because I don't act. For a good reason, I prefer to play myself."[12] Like Autry, Ritter understood that he was first and foremost an entertainer. In this sense "acting" suggested a world removed from that occupied by the audience; as personified by Autry and Ritter, the performance not of character but of "self" recommended a more immediate and tangible relationship with their fans.

With *The Old Corral* the screenwriters provided a scenario that allowed Autry to pit himself against more urbane forms of entertainment and to suggest an implied criticism of metropolitan western singers. The story concerns a night-club singer (Hope Manning) who witnessed a gangland slaying. Sought by both gangsters and the police, she flees west and finds a job singing in a gambling joint. For her debut she wears an elegant evening dress, in marked contrast to the rough and basic setting. Her first number is a sentimental tune in which she practices running up and down the musical scales. The patrons are suitably unimpressed and she breaks into tears. Autry consoles her: "You have a beautiful voice—they're just not educated to that type of music." She suggests that they sing "Heart of the West," with Gene accompanying her on guitar and vocals. The song goes over well with the audience, not because of the simple change from an urban to a western theme but because of Autry's singing. The young woman's voice is almost lost in the mix, which Autry dominates. To force home the point about inappropriate singing and song material, Autry finishes with the solo number "Money Ain't No Use Anyway." It is an upbeat blue yodel song. The choice is telling because the song had no immediate commercial value. Autry had recorded a version five years earlier, in 1931. It represents a throwback to the period when he mimicked Jimmie Rodgers, a style that Autry had pretty much abandoned. The performance functions, then, as a signifier of Autry's immediate roots: a symbol of the tradition that his music and singing draw upon and a counter to the nonvernacular styles of his competitors.[13]

Perhaps the most self-reflexive of Autry's films to engage with his star persona is *The Big Show* (Republic, 1936), which is built around the events of Texas's centennial celebrations and the platforms that it provides for a variety of performance situations. It was designed as an Autry special with guest spots for three of the biggest names in vernacular music making: the Sons of the Pioneers, the Light Crust Doughboys, and the Beverly Hillbillies. It also included cameos for Max Terhune, the cowboy ventriloquist who would eventually be featured as one of Republic's Three Mesquiteers, and the African-American vocal group the Jones Boys; to accommodate these acts the film was ten minutes longer than the usual entries in the Autry series.

The Big Show begins with Autry leading the Beverly Hillbillies in song but undercuts this formulaic opening when the camera rapidly tracks away from the musicians and reveals that they are extras, stuntmen, and bit players in a series western production for "Mammoth Pictures" who are idly making music for themselves. Autry is the stunt double for Tom Ford (also Gene Autry), a series western star and Mammoth's biggest asset. The film differentiates Tom Ford from the stunt-double Autry by Ford's pencil-thin moustaches, his ineptitude with horses, and an arrogance so great that it repels his female costar. After shooting on the western has finished, Ford opts to do some hunting rather than fulfill his contract to appear as a special attraction at the Texas centennial celebrations. Somewhat against his will, though recognizing the costs to Mammoth of Ford's breaking the contract, Autry carries out a successful impersonation. Immediately, the characters offer a poignant contrast—Autry the stuntman *works* and recognizes the responsibility of the star to his audience, while the celluloid cowboy prefers to amuse himself and go on vacation. The plot provides a number of incidents for Autry to prove that he is a "real" cowboy and not the "drugstore" variety that he is accused of being when mistaken for Tom Ford. The film includes a montage of Autry stunts to authenticate his unacknowledged physical superiority but more trenchantly to depict his performances as labor. The sequence begins with images of two cameras and their operators superimposed on each side of the screen;

here, within a low-budget, low-cultural form that targets a working-class audience, the representation of the camera is remarkably similar to one used in Dziga Vertov's Soviet masterpiece, *The Man with a Movie Camera* (1929). Yet the revealing of the film's means of production is clearly not intended as a political technique of "distantiation" to break the spectator's identification with the film.[14] Rather, in this context it incorporates the apparatus of filmmaking to a specific end: to produce a concept of filmmaking as work, production, and labor. While the divergence between the political, social, and economic contexts of a 1930s series western and the revolutionary practice of early Soviet cinema is enormous, both articulate the connection between filmmaking, industrial technologies of cultural production, and proletarian class address. Autry's stuntman persona accrues the benefit of his position within this equation, because it translates into a critique of the male star who has clearly "gone Hollywood" in his abrogation of duties to his audience.[15] The further irony of this self-reflexive episode, however, is that the film signifies Gene Autry's authenticity (as stuntman) through the effacement of the labor of real stuntmen because the montage is composed of scenes from earlier Monogram westerns and the stunts of Yakima Canutt.

The "doubling" of Autry enables the "real" Gene Autry to distance himself from the Hollywood star who has disconnected from his core audience. The structure of the story line establishes the "real" Gene Autry as the true star through his ability to sing. While Autry (while assumed to be Tom Ford) is waiting to appear on a radio show, the station producer overhears him singing and gleefully induces a reluctant Autry to sing on the show. This performance is what definitively differentiates the two characters. In a further heightening of the self-reflexivity of *The Big Show*, the fictional Mammoth's president overhears the radio performance and seizes on the novelty of the singing cowboy, envisioning its commercial success; this is a comic scene that the audience would have recognized as a humorous commentary on Autry's film career.

The desired transparency of relationship between audience and performer is particularly notable in the figure of the sidekick. The comic genius of Autry's sidekick, Smiley Burnette, was integral to the success that Autry's films achieved. Burnette's musical talent was as great as his clowning skills, and each film at some point provided him with a showcase. Generally, these spots highlighted his ability to play any number of instruments, often of a homemade variety. In this he echoed Frank Norris's blackface minstrels in *McTeague*—men who could "wrestle a tune out of almost anything. . . . McTeague was stupefied with admiration. 'That's what you call musicians,' he announced gravely. 'Home Sweet Home,' played upon the trombone. Think of that! Art could go no further."[16]

If Burnette was following a vaudeville tradition in his use of found objects to produce his music, he was also paving the way for other entertainers. The Hoosier Hot Shots and then Spike Jones and his City Slickers later made careers out of comically deconstructing the musical hits of the day.[17] White jazz bands such as the Original Dixieland Jazz Band and Ladd's Black Aces had partly filled the historical continuity between blackface multi-instrumentalists and Burnette. This humorous "nut jazz" had, as the jazz historian William Howland Kenney writes, a lasting impact on social dance music that emphasized an "overtly comical form of syncopated dance music." The Paul Biese College Inn Orchestra, for example, "played tunes like 'Bow Wow,' 'Chili Bean,' 'Timbuctoo,' 'Happy Hottentot,' and 'Dardenella' with a clearly delineated saxophone melody adorned by a broadly slapstick tailgate trombone, laughing muted trumpet, and squealing clarinet."[18] Black and white rural music, as played by jug and hokum bands, respectively, also replicated this comical musical performance. Despite the western context, Burnette's musical performances often lean toward nut jazz. His idiosyncratic vocal style bears considerable comparison with the coon singer 'Gene Greene, who billed himself as the "Ragtime King." Burnette's early recordings, such as "Deep Froggy Blues" (1937), sound uncannily similar to Greene's 1917 recording "King of the Bungaloos."[19] Indeed, one of Burnette's biggest musical influences appears to have been Cab Calloway. This is clear from Burnette's wonderful 1935 recording, "Minnie the Moocher at the Morgue," a mix of Calloway's tune and the blues standard "St. James Infirmary," and Burnette's rendition of "Heebie Jeebie Blues" in *Public Cowboy #1* (Republic, 1937).[20] Autry also recorded the occasional jazz-inflected number such as "Down in the Land of Zulu" (minstrelsy with a crawling snake clarinet accompaniment), which backs Smiley's drag act in *Spring Time in the Rockies*. As with Autry, Burnette effortlessly mixed the old with new.

The sidekick is an American original. He is not the western's version of a court jester, whose function was to offer an inverted image of the monarch—a means for "absolute power to practice humility."[21] The sidekick's basic function was to keep the hero in the realm of the com-

Smiley Burnette

mon man, not to confirm his preeminence. However much the court
jester offers himself as a point of comparison, the sidekick draws his
tomfoolery not from the courts of medieval Europe but from the clowns
of blackface minstrelsy. In most of Burnette's performances the minstrel heritage is all but invisible. However, at moments the play with performance and comedy are explicitly indebted to blackface. In *Round
Up Time in Texas* (Republic, 1937) Burnette plays the final third of the
film entirely in blackface, a conceit justified by the film's "African" setting. Autry and Burnette have traveled to Dunbar, South Africa, with a
consignment of horses, and the police mistake them for criminal diamond buyers; Autry and Burnette escape from jail, only to be captured
by tribesmen. In order to effect an escape Burnette disguises himself
by blacking up with the soot from the outside of an old cooking pot.
In *Carolina Moon* (Republic, 1940) Burnette appears simultaneously in
drag and blackface, justified by the film's plantation setting. But despite
drawing upon these older traditions in his musical and comic performances, the sidekick was a unique character type whose importance to
the audience of the series western cannot be overestimated.

Inevitably, toward the end of an Autry film Frog Millhouse yells out, after falling from the back of a truck or carriage, "Hey, wait for me!" The audience would not have been concerned for him, for it knows he will always catch up with the action and for most of the film had helped to drive it along. He may at times appear backward—an idea expressed by the repetition from film to film of Smiley's riding his horse or mule facing its rear end—but it is a deception that the villains are always late in discovering. In an act of comic self-reflexivity in *Public Cowboy #1*, Smiley first appears singing "Flop Eared Mule," which contains the line "I'm always wandering, going nowhere," and wearing a mask on the back of his head—so he can see in front and behind. This cowboy Janus figure is no man's servant or master; he is a wise fool whose lack of deference to established authority figures is broadly and generally evoked across the spectrum of 1930s series westerns.

The sidekick's comedic antics punctuate the formulaic narrative of flight, pursuit, capture, and escape as much as the music interludes do. Smiley Burnette's principal function is to act as the comic foil to Autry. "Rules and Regulations Made and Observed by Cowboy Star," publicity material for *Rootin' Tootin' Rhythm*, note that "a western hero can never be 'funny.' You can laugh with him, but never at him."[22] But the splitting of the two types of humor between lead and sidekick reflects more than just protocol for preserving the dignity and authority of the lead. Burnette's comedic spectacles are not simply unmotivated or spontaneous events but enact responses to problems that the narrative initiates. This is particularly marked when Smiley's drag act symbolically stabilizes gender conventions that the film has unsettled.

In *Tumbling Tumbleweeds* the heavies call Autry a "lavender cowboy," an obvious insinuation of effeminacy and homosexuality. Evidently putting his masculinity into question, the film requires a restoration of Autry's properly "manly" gender identity, and Smiley's function is to provide a space within which to do this. Autry desists from violent confrontation with his accusers, choosing instead to outwit them. Though quite capable of such physical engagement, Autry's recourse to means other than violence to solve problems clearly contradicts dominant constructions of an idealized masculinity. This sets up a struggle between forms of masculinity that runs throughout Autry's films: his extravagant cowboy apparel and outsider status as a musician might be said to feminize him. Yet Autry's exceptionality lies in his clear construction as the object of female desire, both within the film and outside it, although he does not participate in the particular conception of masculinity shared by the heavies. Nonetheless, a number of films "resolve" the conflict around versions of heterosexual masculinity through Burnette's more overtly performative "drag" plays with gender and dress. As "Little Egypt" in *Guns and Guitars,* as a "Mammy" in *Carolina Moon,* as a spinster in *Oh, Susanna!* and in *Springtime in the Rockies* (Republic, 1937), where he performs his impersonation of femininity with the aid of a skirt made from a lamp shade, Smiley in drag is not simply a comic excursion across gender boundaries but a means by which to deflect concerns about Autry's effeminacy. Burnette's transvestite routine is hyperbolic excess that marks out "true" gender inversion. As it is literally unthinkable for Autry to move into the space of the sidekick ("to be laughed at"), he also is ideologically proscribed from transgressing gender boundaries. Set against Burnette's immersion in "feminine" identity, Autry's identity seems unimpeachably male. The force of the "lavender cowboy" jibe rests on Autry's fancy costumes—Burnette's drag act serves to give the lie to the accusation that it is Autry who has cross-dressed.

Competing plays between traditionally male- and newly female-defined versions of masculinity illustrate the centrality of women to Autry—in his audience, in his films, and in the making of his films. In his autobiography he states:

> The leading ladies in Autry films were not there just for decoration or to point out which way the bad guys went. As written, they gave me a lot of anything-you-can-do-I-can-do-better sass, smoked a lot of Kools— that era's Virginia Slims and, in general, played a thirties' version of waiting for Gloria (Steinem). That may have been due, in no small part, to the presence of such screenwriters as Betty Burbridge, Luci Ward, and Connie Lee. We didn't exactly use them because they were experts on the West. Whatever their formula, those films were about the only ones in the B Western category, up to then, that had a mass appeal to women.[23]

The studio often publicized the use of female writers for Autry films, notably in an advertisement for Smith-Corona typewriters that ran in the *Saturday Evening Post.* The ad shows Autry alongside Burbridge, and the copy emphasizes the role that Smith-Corona typewriters play in her successful career.[24] Whether it was as scriptwriters, as the most significant part of his audience, or in their roles within his films, women were crucial to Autry's success. Remarkably for a genre considered to be of exclusively male interest, the neglected singing western offers exceptional material for cultural studies concerned with women's roles in the historical formation and reformation of gendered identities.

"Although love interest in Gene's pictures is negligible, most of his fan mail comes from girls in their teens and early twenties," wrote Mary Barnsley, a reporter for the Associated Press. "Doesn't this prompt you to put more romance into your pictures?" she asked him. Autry's reply was short and brisk no.[25] In a long interview another reporter asked Betty Burbridge how she approached the writing of Autry's scripts: "Naturally in writing stories around Gene, I must consider all ages and sexes, and treat the romantic angle very lightly."[26] Though romance might alienate the youngsters in the audience, it did not exclude lengthy musical numbers in which Autry uses the song to express emotions he is not able to show physically. The film's dependence on music to express physical and emotional desire means that Autry conforms to an ideal of romantic love that exists outside the physical, where the man holds women in reverence and respects them. As yet another reporter put it, "There is something about a Western man . . . that makes a woman feel that she is on that well-known pedestal once again. They have a gift for making a woman feel like a saint."[27] The journalist's suggestion that cowboys like Gene Autry place women on high "once again" perhaps answers the question posed by another journalist—"Why Gene Autry receives gobs of fan mail from expectant mothers we will never understand. But receive it he does."[28]

However, Autry's films were not inured from the radical shifts in social and sexual mores that had challenged old-fashioned ideas of femininity by the 1930s. While journalists used the language of the Victorian angel of the hearth and the romantic virgin on a pedestal, the films' depictions of women conform more closely to images of the New Woman of modernity—educated, independent, and fashionable. Crucially, hedonistic sexual expressiveness is not part of the language of independence of Autry's female leads, which differentiates them from modernity's emblematic New Woman, the jazz baby, or flapper, of the 1920s. Rather, the women in Autry's films forge their connections with modernity, perhaps ambivalently, through the worlds of work and of consumption. In other words, the Victorian and romantic archetypes of femininity are profoundly historicized in narratives rooted in the social and economic upheavals of the depression.

In his analysis of the left wing's cultural response to this period, Michael Denning writes, "If the Depression years were not a moment of feminist militancy, they were surely a time of gender strife and change: many commentators at the time noted the crisis in masculinity that accompanied the massive unemployment of the depression."[29] The intimate threads tying work, economic responsibility, family authority, and social stability to definitions of masculinity were clearly unraveling. In Autry's films, and other series westerns, rapacious capitalism often emasculates the ranchers and farmers as producers. The background for considering the representation of women is this destabilization of traditional gender roles. It is noteworthy, then, that against time-honored stereotyping the young female leads of the mid- to late 1930s are independent wage earners, managers, or property owners. A female character's entry into the world of ownership and productive employment often entails responsibility for a family formed in the absence of a mother and characterized by weak men: an ailing father and/ or a younger or weaker brother. The film critic Richard Maltby identifies this narrative scenario as specific to the depression and says it is to be found in some of the films most successful at the box office, particularly those starring Deanna Durbin and Shirley Temple.[30] Women's displacement of men from the sphere of work and familial authority may be registering precisely the patriarchal "crisis" that Denning identifies. The films modify presentation of a woman as active, independent, and in control of her own destiny by showing that her responsibility for the younger or enfeebled male pushes her into the public arena. In the classic case her public visibility leaves her open to the predations of the villain from which the hero must protect her. This suggests that, along with fulfilling the fantasy of rescue, the hero delimits the woman's independence and activity with the restitution of patriarchal authority. I believe that yet a stronger case can be made that the requirement for such closure does not motivate the appearance of strongly independent women within the films. What is striking in these films is precisely how unmotivated and "natural" the independent and economically active woman is: the films do not mark her as extraordinary, and her position passes without comment. Further, they do not present the absence of a mother as a vacancy awaiting the daughter's occupancy; these are not narratives in which independent women appear in the realm of the public in order to be "rightfully" returned to a solely domestic life by the end. Countering examples of women in series westerns with complex family responsibilities are ample instances of female leads without any kinship complications, such as those of Tex Ritter's *Riders of the Rockies* and *Trouble in Texas* (both released by Grand National in 1937). In these both female leads play undercover government agents who use the disguise of saloon entertainer to work their way into the villain's confidence. The ploy enables the women's infiltration of the criminal fraternity, but, more pointedly, their assumption of the lowly status of saloon girl legitimizes their appearance within this homosocial sphere. As government agents institutionally empowered to capture criminal men, the female leads occupy positions of social authority; as showgirls, they are reduced in power through the cultural association of perform-ing women with wanton sexuality (as typified in film by Marlene Die-trich). The performances, although revealed as subterfuge and bound-ed by audience knowledge of the duplicity, nonetheless exploit the sexual objectification of women performers to offer the film audience the vicarious pleasures of female display. Accordingly, the films ambiv-alently encode their song-and-dance acts, presenting them as deceptive spectacle of female performance in which the performers "are" and "are not" the women they appear to be. Such dissembling play around public music performance patently acknowledges that women perform-ers could enter into the cowboy's world but that conservative ideolo-gies of gender and female sexuality would dictate the terms of access.

Until the development in the early 1930s of the singing cowgirl, the space for female performers within the developing white rural music industry was limited to roles within family acts, best exemplified by the Carter Family. Mary A. Bufwack and Robert K. Oermann, his-torians of women in country music, calculated that only 5 percent of professional or semiprofessional performers were women, and most worked in family groups.[31] The male figure in the group helped legit-imize the public appearance of the women by acting as a paternal chaperone, discouraging perception of female performers as socially abject. However, not all female performers conformed to this gender configuration. Working with two of the biggest names in early commer-cial rural music, Vernon Dalhart and Carson Robison, Adelyne Hood assumed the role of a female rounder and often used a western per-sona. On her recording of "Calamity Jane" (1929) she brags: "When it comes to drinking likker, I can take a dozen men / And drink 'em under the table and up on the chairs again."[32] But Hood, who also recorded "coon songs," was a rarity among early female performers and clearly relied upon the spaces created by turn-of-the-century female coon singers, such as May Irwin and Sophie Tucker, who, like Mae West, for all their celebration of female strength, represented a déclassé and wanton femininity.

The popularity of the *National Barn Dance* with a female audience encouraged the producers to engage an ever-increasing roster of women performers. The most successful was Patsy Montana, who began her career imitating Jimmie Rodgers's blue yodels in talent contests. In 1933 she joined up with the Prairie Ramblers, one of the finest prewar string bands, and began to make appearances on WLS. By then she had been making personal appearances for at least two years as a cowgirl. As with the shift by male performers from rounders and hillbillies to cowboys, the role of cowgirl proved equally acceptable to a broad audience. Bufwack and Oermann suggest that it "rolled the sweetheart and tomboy into one, giving traditional values an updated image."[33] Following on the heels of Patsy Montana at WLS were the Girls from the Golden West, a sister duo. An interviewer in the late 1970s asked one sister how successful they might have been if they had billed themselves and their music as hillbilly. She answered by suggesting that that type of music was "rangy, tangy, real harsh, and I didn't think we were like that."[34] In other words, hillbilly music and its image were not respectable, but being a cowgirl, with its mix of the new and the old, of independence and conformity, movement and stasis, domesticity and fugitiveness, was both daring and respectable. Patsy Montana's song "I Wanna Be a Cowboy's Sweetheart" summed this up: despite its title, the song suggests the woman's desire to partake in pleasures more often seen as masculine.

Toward the end of its existence Grand National released a news item announcing that Harry Dreifuss was planning an "all-girl Western."[35] That idea did not materialize, but the studio did produce three singing westerns starring Dorothy Page: *Ride 'Em Cowgirl* (1938), *Water Rustlers* (1939), and *The Singing Cowgirl* (1939). The studio's perilous finances meant these were underresourced pictures, and other studios did not pick up the novelty.

Though somewhat overdetermined in its emphasis on women as signifiers of modernity and change with its four college-educated female characters, *Springtime in the Rockies* (Republic, 1937) is broadly representative of women in Autry's oeuvre. Autry is the foreman on a ranch bequeathed to Sandra Knight (Polly Rowles). Though recently graduated from a Chicago college with a diploma in animal husbandry, she has no practical experience in ranching. With three classmates in tow she intends to try out "modern scientific methods" to counter "antediluvian ideas about cattle raising." From the outset, when the women are suckered into buying a flock of sheep, the film gently mocks their attempts at scientific management and restates the gendered adage that abstract knowledge cannot replace knowledge gained through physical, practical experience. The point of the film, however, is not to demean the value of education nor to denigrate the women's use of education to enter into the male world of work. Rather, it is to moderate the distance between the far-off world of modern "expert" professionalization and that of local, traditional competence in husbandry. The women are not humiliated; instead, their engaged enthusiasm, which positively mediates their lack of experience, seems to offer a starting point for their ambitions. In other words, the film is not a reactionary tale that attempts to neutralize the "threat" of the new modern woman; the film signifies the female characters as agents of change, yet processes that accommodate them within Autry's West avert potential for wholesale disruption. The chief means of doing this is their adoption of the dress of the cowgirl, which symbolically balances the claims of the old and the new.

Before their adoption of the costume of the cowgirl at a Pioneers' Day dance, the film has readily reduced the women's appearances to the visual characteristics of the bookish brunette with spectacles, the slightly dizzy blond (who plays a ukelele), and the overweight tomboy. Sandra Knight is neither mousy nor glamorous, bookish nor superficially attractive. By donning the cowgirl costumes, the women lose their somewhat dowdy and decidedly unromantic look and assume a more conventionally attractive appearance. This marks a transition from the asexual urban and modern look they bring from Chicago to the sexually attractive and, in this context, contemporary image of the cowgirl more suited to Autry's West. Smiley's drag act, which accompanies their impromptu stage debut at the dance, once again echoes the passage toward desirable gender identity through costuming; here it serves as a comic underscoring of the women's assumption of a western identity.

Beyond their function as signifiers of a moderate modernity within the film, the four women also provide points at which they become idealized surrogates for Autry's extrafilmic female audience. The first scene in which this is evident shows the four women lying head to head in bed in a dilapidated bunkhouse and listening as if to the radio but actually to Autry singing outside. The second scene in which they play the role of audience surrogates is when Autry and Sandra are touring the ranch and stop to listen to cowboys singing as they work; unbeknown to the couple, one of Sandra's pals is up a tree with binoculars, spying on her and Autry. As relayed to the other two friends on the ground below, her commentary on their activities is a humorous take on the failure of the observed actuality to match the idolizing fan's starry-eyed expectations of Autry as romantic lead.

The Big Show gives even stronger acknowledgment of the pleasures of fandom for what it calls Autry's "snooping female" audience. A horde of female fans mistakes Autry for Hollywood star Tom Ford, pulls him from his horse, and literally strips the clothes from his body. Autry's startled dismay at this dimension of "star" treatment is wonderfully modest: "I don't mind being run over in stampedes, falling over cliffs or fighting wild animals, but when a bunch of women tear my clothes off—I quit!" What is clear in these scenes is that whether as listeners to his radio shows, viewers of his films, or in the fantasy objectification of Autry's body and the fan's fetishization of his costumes, women are being positioned as active consumers of "Gene Autry." This recognizes a second major dimension of women as bearers of modernity. The representation of independent women acting as free agents within the world of work implicitly acknowledges the massive economic and social changes that accompanied the shift from rural to fully industrialized production in the early decades of the twentieth century. The female characters are, in this sense, emblematic of modernity's transformations. As modern women, however, it is equally true that their connections with the world of modernity are effected through displays of consumption that, historically, were increasingly being defined as "feminine."

The dual construction of the modernity of the female lead of *Blue Montana Skies* (Republic, 1939) is particularly marked. The setting for much of the film's action is the dude ranch owned by Dorothy (June Storey), which she has turned from a barely viable cattle ranch into a successful site for vacationing city dwellers. Having installed her as economically commanding, the plot does not question her independence, which also is not the "problem" that the film must "solve." Yet, as an entrepreneur of the modern, Dorothy oversees a business of which the principal product is the consumption of leisure. And opportunities for female display, which are inextricably tied to consumption practices, punctuate her role as the working woman. In particular she acts as a mannequin for consumer items: makeup, hairstyle, and, of course, her clothes. Republic's press books often supplied stories that emphasized this point: "June Storey was particularly happy about her role opposite Gene Autry . . . because the film provides her with a chance to display feminine fashions. Usually June wears cute western outfits in her outdoor films, but this role allowed her fashions, dear to her feminine heart."[36] Unlike the other characters, the female lead goes through a number of costume changes. To give it significance modeling the latest fashions demands a space for public spectacle outside the confines of the domestic. It is not unreasonable to extrapolate from this the suggestion that female leads' captivity within circuits of consumption is the price for their release from the domestic. This neatly parallels the findings of studies that argue that cinema in the 1930s was instrumental in tutoring women in consumer-appropriate ways of channeling feminine desire.[37]

Given the contradictory strands constituting female identity in the series western—Victorian and modern, romantic and independent, active and passive, producer and consumer—the future for the couple at the end of a series western is ambivalent. Because the audience is not homogeneous, various interpretations of the closure are available. Boys and girls might construe it less as the formation of the romantic couple than as a temporary full stop: the independent hero and heroine will return again to struggle against the odds. Men and women, though, could read the final clinch as a closure that suits either party's desires—either independent or conforming woman, either unpossessive or dominant male. The open endedness of the final scene is symptomatic of a film form that eschews closure through a one-dimensional resolution of conflict. Indeed, what might ordinarily be "tensions" between men and women—about individuality, possession, ownership, and control—are conspicuously absent. More broadly, such refusals of neatly defined positions typifies the series western. The presentation of other important relations—between old and new, capital and labor, rural and urban—rejects simple polarization. The best way to further explore the absence of this tension is through the ways in which these films use emblems of disguise and masking as metaphors for the instabilities of cultural, social, and economic transformation.

SIX

New Deal Cowboys: The Mystery of the Hooded Riders

Carrying all the ingredients that make a punchy Western for children, this one adds a topical touch to entice grown ups. . . . Rathmell's screenplay spatters mild political satire among the colloquialisms.

> —*Hollywood Reporter* review of Tex Ritter in *Song of the Buckaroo* (Monogram, 1938)

We don't recognize your law, Judge.

> —*Guns of the Pecos* (Warner Bros., 1937)

"A popular situation which adds zest to the climax" of series westerns, notes a *New York Times* reporter, "is that in which the hero poses as a bad man and conceals his sterling qualities until the end."[1] The play with identity via masquerades is endemic to the series western. The use of disguise is manifested in character reversals by the villain, who poses as friend and helper to the persecuted, and by the hero, who works undercover as a crook to reveal the villain's nefarious plot. These disguises are overly transparent and clearly recognizable as such to the series western's audience. The final act revealing the villain and hero is always anticlimactic. The audience has never had any real doubt about their "true" identity.

The unfolding of the plot is not what maintains interest. The meaning lies in the act itself. Series and singing westerns' involvement with "borrowed costumes and assumed accents" is performance *and* metaphor. As performance, series westerns borrow from traditions of popular entertainment that have a long history: low forms of theatrical melodrama, vaudeville and burlesque skits and musical exhibitions, circus acts, medicine and Wild West shows, and blackface minstrelsy. As metaphor, the series western's dramatic use of disguise, masking, and hidden and mistaken identity is not, principally, the "sign of an enigma to be solved" but rather "a narrative equivalent of metaphor," as Michael Denning notes of the use of disguise in dime novels.[2] Characters in the series western are not naturalistic figures in a fictional equivalent of the world inhabited by its audience but are instead its fantasized substitutes who act out the audience's fears and desires. Through the donning of disguises, characters in series westerns—the outlaw who is in fact a lawman, for example—perform as metaphors for specific social, cultural, and economic struggles.

The performance of disguise and hidden identity reveals the films as rehearsing an old but still relevant story of the individual's uncertain place within the republic of the United States. The U.S. Constitution promises equality alongside the understanding that the citizen pays deference to nobody. However, the self-evident inequalities that confronted working-class Americans profoundly contradicted such egalitarianism, particularly for those who had to abandon self-employment for example, a landowning farmer—and who subsequently took up wage labor. That is, autonomous citizens would now have to be mind ful of the demands of their boss—as workers employed by a company; the "free" citizen would be compromised. Popular nineteenth-century working-class entertainment, such as dime novels and blackface minstrelsy, restaged the contradiction between the republic's promise of deference to no one and the lived reality of wage labor.

Westerns were allegories on the state of the nation, and their audience recognized them as such. This process of "reading" has much in common with Denning's theory about the dime novel as allegory. He suggests that this particular fictional world is "less a representation of the real world than a microcosm. . . . Individual characters are less individuals than figures for social groups."[3] He continues: "This allegorical mode of reading depends upon the existence of a master plot by which to read the disguises; and that master plot was in working class cultures of the nineteenth-century the story of the Republic itself. The stories of individuals and of individual families become types of the citizens of the Republic, both in utopian images of its fulfillment as the co-operative commonwealth and in the stories of its betrayal, as it becomes a land of tramps and millionaires."[4] The case that Denning makes about popular culture and workers of the late nineteenth century is equally applicable to culture and workers well into the twentieth century. Narratives of a betrayed but finally saved republic run throughout the series westerns of the 1930s, a narrative conceit that owed much to the magnification of social divisions engendered by the Great Depression. Both series westerns and dime novels act out reconciliation of the contradiction between the needs of the individual and the demands of living and working in a modern economy.

This act of reconciliation is significant because, as the historian Alan Trachtenberg has argued, in the late nineteenth and well into the twentieth century, labor thought of itself as upholding "nothing so much as the fundamental American traditions of republicanism and equality." Indeed, labor believed it had "the most authentic voice of America."[5] However, the "voice" of labor did not have access to an effective mass media forum outside popular entertainment and fictions. The struggle with inequality and class division that took place within these divertissements assumed the disguise of allegory. Discussing this phenomenon as it occurs in dime novels, Denning writes: "If historical struggles do take place in borrowed costumes and assumed accents, if social and economic divisions appear in disguise, then the source for these disguises and the manifestation of these roles lie in the conventional characters of a society, played out in its popular narratives."[6]

The "metaphor of disguise" invariably instructs the narrative concerns of series westerns, and its various conceits and their deployment ensure a "loose" plot structure that is able to contain the many digressive performance sequences that guarantee a level of novelty while being sufficiently "focused" to enable the repeated telling of the story of a world turned upside down. Take, for example, Autry's *Rootin' Tootin' Rhythm,* which is nothing out of the ordinary in its use of disguise. A rash of rustling has plagued local ranchers; the only herd not affected is Autry's. Under the ruse that they are out-of-work cowboys, Texas Rangers (Al Clauser and His Oklahoma Outlaws) find employment on Autry's ranch. However, they drop their suspicion of Autry's involvement in the rustling ring after someone steals his herd. Autry appears unperturbed by the incident and goes to bed rather than chase after the rustlers. But this is an act so that he can leave the ranch undetected and pursue the rustlers on his own, though events conspire to team him with Smiley. On the trail of the rustlers Gene and Smiley find the bodies of two deputies gunned down by two notorious outlaws. The outlaws have swapped clothes with the deputies, and now Gene and Smiley exchange their apparel for the outlaws'. Their appearance now matches the images of the outlaws on "Wanted" posters. At this point in the narrative the agents of the law, the Rangers, are masquerading as cowboys, two killers are masquerading as lawmen, and Autry and Burnette are masquerading as outlaws. The latters' subterfuge is successful: upon entering a saloon, Autry confirms that they are bad men by ordering a drink of straight whiskey and a rye chaser, but, needless to say, neither he nor Smiley consumes these drinks. Autry attends a meeting of the cattlemen's association, which is debating the need for a vigilante committee. A rancher identifies Autry as the infamous Apache Kid, and Gene and Smiley, pursued by a posse, hightail it out of town. Autry had intended that his performance as an outlaw would gain the attention of the rustlers, who would then take him into their confidence. Much to Smiley's amazement, the head of the rustlers is also the head of the cattlemen's association, but Autry is less incredulous: "Why of course! Can you think of a better way for the head of a rustlers' ring to cover up?" However, Autry's ruse is confounded when the real Apache Kid appears, an event that momentarily forestalls the end of the film and allows Autry's real identity to be revealed to the female lead so that they can work together to see that justice has its day. The outlaws and the rustlers are caught, and Gene, Smiley, and the Rangers' true identities are confirmed as legitimate. These exchanges of identities are not just to enable plot development; rather, the play with disguise and hidden identity construct a world turned upside down, at least initially: spokesmen for the community are actually the chief threat to its well-being (the head of the cattlemen's association who is also the head of the rustlers), outlaws are lawmen (Apache Kid in the deputy's clothes), honest citizens are outlaws (Autry and Burnette masquerading as Apache Kid and his sidekick), and lawmen are workers (the Rangers masquerade as cowboys). By its end the film has transformed this inverted world, and the power that was once lodged with the corrupt has been returned to where it rightly belongs, with the people.

The play with disguise is particularly apparent in the series of "outlaw" films that starred Roy Rogers. In *Billy the Kid Returns* (Republic, 1938) Rogers plays both Billy the Kid and "himself." The story concerns the threat by the big rancher, Morgenson, to run the homesteaders off their land. Taking the basic story elements of the myth of Billy the Kid, the film begins with Billy and his gang in McSween's store, holding out against Morgenson and his men, who have surrounded and set fire to the place. Despite overwhelming odds, Billy escapes the inferno. The following scenes neatly encapsulate the two sides of Billy—killer and helper of the poor: taking a horse, Billy coldbloodedly shoots its owner, but while on the run he takes time out to help a widow threatened by the villain's henchmen. Explaining his actions, Billy tells her that his father had been a homesteader. Later that night Pat Garrett stalks and finally kills Billy.

After Billy's death the film cuts to Roy Rogers, who is riding and singing "Born to the Saddle"—"with a song on my lips." Meanwhile, Morgenson's cronies are trying to drive out another family of homesteaders. They steal the family's horses and set fire to their house. Hearing gunshots, Roy rides to the scene, where he encounters the thieves. Because they think he is Billy the Kid, they ride off in fright. Rounding up the horses, Roy drives them back to the homestead, where Frog Millhouse has turned up with a caravan of musicians and his stock of Dixie Brand musical instruments. Frog and Roy are old Texas school pals, so he knows Roy is not Billy, but no one believes them, despite their protestations.

While in town buying the burned-out homesteader's kids ice cream, the sheriff arrests Frog and Roy. Attempting to prove his identity as an out-of-work peace officer (he had been fired from his last job because he was thought to be too young for the responsibility), Roy sings a song, for everyone knows that Billy did not have a musical pulse in his whole body. Frog and Roy perform a duet, "Wonder Why I Feel So Happy." Because there is a reward for Billy, the citizens who arrested Roy still believe he is Billy the Kid. However, the dispute ends when Garrett turns up and explains that Roy cannot be Billy, as he has just killed him.

Earlier, a government representative had confronted the marshal and demanded that he protect the homesteaders. However, as federal employees, the law officer is powerless to intercede in a local issue. The marshal explains that Billy the Kid had been more effective than the law at policing Morgenson and his gang. The solution is to deputize Roy Rogers, who will then impersonate Billy the Kid, effectively becoming both law officer and outlaw.

Garrett is uncertain of Roy's abilities as he too believes Rogers to be too young and inexperienced and that he will soon turn from helping the poor to robbing the rich, just like Billy. Nevertheless, they go ahead with the ruse, and a montage of newspaper headlines informs the viewer of "Billy's" exploits: "BILLY THE KID ESCAPES, RANCHERS ROUTED BY BILLY THE KID—OUTLAW BREAKS UP CAMPAIGN AGAINST NESTERS, HOMESTEADERS SWARMING INTO LINCOLN COUNTY—END OF OPEN RANGE PREDICTED." "Read that, Pat," the marshal tells Garrett. "Life and property safe again—all because an outlaw's doing our job." Complications follow when Roy is thought to have truly turned outlaw after taking a storekeeper's money, which he had, but he did so in order to protect it and not for his own benefit.

Rogers's masquerade as Billy the Kid repositions the myth of Robin Hood (who stole from the rich to give to the poor), which the stories told of Billy the Kid had appropriated. This allows Rogers paradoxically to legitimatize the outlaw. In effect, the film uses the outlaw's unfettered ability to take action in order to solve a problem that recognized law officers had been unable to resolve. This particular play with disguise reinforces the myth of the outlaw as a friend of the downtrodden while mitigating those aspects of outlawry—the coldblooded killings and self-interest—that in turn militate against the outlaw as a legitimate protector of the populace. Having Billy played by a law officer dissolves the accusation of glorifying the outlaw.

In *The Days of Jesse James* (Republic, 1939) Rogers again assumes the disguise of the outlaw. Roy is a police officer employed by the Bankers' Association. His job is to find out who is behind the robbery of the Wyatt brothers' bank in Missouri. The suspects are Jesse James and his gang, so Roy and his sidekick assume the identity of outlaws in order to infiltrate the gang. The film peddles the familiar myth about Jesse's being driven into a life of crime by railroad corporations yet a person committed to the community and family—Jesse is a good man gone bad. Unlike Rogers's earlier film invoking Billy the Kid, *The Days of Jesse James* does not show the outlaw as a killer, and he is not killed in the course of the film. Roy's assumption of Jesse's identity toward the end of the film constitutes yet another inversion of the prevailing order. As viewers have known throughout, the banker Wyatt, who had earlier decried "glorifying outlaws," is finally revealed as the villain. He catches a train that Roy, posing as Jesse, holds up. Roy takes back the loot that the banker has stolen from his depositors and redistributes it among those who had been left destitute after the bank closed. Once again those who appear to be legitimate turn out to be scoundrels, while society's renegades and outsiders are legitimated and affirmed.

It would be a mistake to conclude that such masquerades within series westerns demand a credulous and uncritical audience to accomplish the character exchanges convincingly. This would be to miss the critical point that, *for the audience,* there is no "confusion" about who is who: crucially, the myriad shifts in identities are always wholly transparent to viewers. It is, therefore, a class-based construction to conceive of historical audiences as naive children (unable to rise above the level of the literal) in order to account for the pleasures of textual forms that depart from the conventions of narrative realism. Beyond the immediate plot exchanges, then, disguise is a structuring presence that works, as Denning has argued for its use in nineteenth-century dime novels, to permit characters to move across social, class, and even racial and gender boundaries.

The scholar Bill Brown's reading of dime novels supports the view that the theatrical nature of disguise "establishes character as an abstract role that any 'person' can play." The artifice of identity enables the "violation of the middle-class status quo," which presumes that identities are fixed.[7] In a similar manner blackface minstrelsy had also essayed this fluidity of identity. Autry and the other singing cowboys were the heirs to a century-old performance tradition that enabled the traversing of otherwise fixed identities. As blackface minstrels, white men could cross not only the line between races but also those between classes and genders. As the cultural studies scholars Annemarie Bean and Eric Lott have argued, in the figures of the pantomime or burlesque "wench" and the "highly stylized and costumed near-white woman" or the "prima donna," minstrelsy continued its common project of feminizing blackness.[8] Michael Rogin and David R. Roediger, also cultural studies scholars, contend that the blackface mask is a device of assimilation that enabled marginalized groups, such as Jewish and Irish immigrants, to claim both a symbolic and a literal whiteness as defined against the black Other of minstrelsy and the black bodies that minstrelsy purports to represent.[9] But, as the musicologist Dale Cockrell suggests, minstrelsy's play with fluid identities subverted "'knowing' gained through image—the eye is drawn to representation, which might not be the real—just as a Western mask is not really as it appears: it conceals and promises reordering."[10] While blackface female impersonation, in either the figure of the wench or prima donna, carries its "inevitable quotient of demeaning attributes" and its "opposing urge to authenticity" (as W. T. Lhamon Jr. claims for minstrel performance as a whole), in its "radical portion" it highlights "contamination, literal overlap, and identification with [the] muddier process" of self-generating identities.[11] By arguing that the mask of blackface minstrelsy does not fix identity but instead puts it into continuous play so that liminality is its defining characteristic, Cockrell and Lhamon challenge the argument put forward by Rogin and Roediger, that the blackness of minstrelsy is about "eager replacement of ethnicity or Jewishness with whiteness."[12] Rather, as Lhamon claims, blackface stages "continual transactions of assimilation."[13]

Lhamon has argued that the mask of burnt cork did not simply turn the white performer black for his audience but rather kept the two identities—black and white—continually in play. Either aspect can dominate, depending on the needs of the performance. Looked at in one way, the minstrel is white; looked at in another fashion, he is black; he is then neither black nor white but both: "The minstrel mask . . . enabled viewers to see and performers to show in one figure the connections between working whites and disdained blacks. It compacted together the showing and seeing of sameness along with difference. They appeared to dawn from and on each other. That is to say, the blackface mask allowed young white callows to see themselves in the hounded image of the free/escaped black continually on the lam."[14] As Lhamon shows, the performance, in addition to fostering identification with blackness, can aid in the "belittling" of blackness. But the liberational *and* racist implications of blackface performance need not detain us here because what is germane to Lhamon's model is the idea of identifying with those who are free but yet not free. In the literature on blackface minstrelsy Lhamon is unique in noting that the caricatured black was not a plantation slave but a fugitive. Whether as a freeman or escaped slave, he was always on the run.[15] This image held a powerful pull for minstrelsy's young white male audiences, who made up a large part of the fluid and mobile U.S. workforce. The "wandering instability" of the minstrel mirrors his audience's unease with the vagaries of wage labor: tied to an often unhealthy and life-threatening factory job, the laborer is also threatened by summary dismissal.

Like the minstrel figure on the lam, the cowboy is able to assume a number of contradictory faces. His actions help to confirm the importance of a sedentary life—domesticity—but his constant roaming would appear to undermine or forgo this way of living. This paradox is often neatly contained within the films' endings, where the young heroine whose ranch has been saved rides away with the hero. She has not given up her ranch, nor has the hero forsworn domesticity. The ending with hero and heroine linked together suggests, rather, that they are both free to move and yet have established a safe place that they can call home. Such an ending combines movement and stasis in a manner similar to the combining of the outlaw and the peace officer. The viewer may isolate either aspect or keep both aspects in view simultaneously. In its own way, this unwillingness to assume a given position either inside or outside society or as a fugitive or sedentary figure challenges the middle-class status quo just as surely as it upsets notions of an absolute patriarchal hierarchy.

The areas of performance and disguise draw on traditional elements within popular culture and tie the series western to its antecedents. But the films were also concerned with contemporary realities, to a far greater degree than they have been given credit for. Despite their circumscribed critiques, series westerns of the 1930s address themselves to the issues of class struggle and division that surfaced during this turbulent decade, at least as much as the more prestigious films of the major studios. The critically disparaged and apparently simplistic genre of the series western has, in its own way, more to say about the social disruptions of capitalism in crisis than such better-known films of the era as *Mr. Deeds Goes to Town* (Columbia, 1936) or *The Grapes of Wrath* (Twentieth Century–Fox, 1940).

However broadly, series westerns focused upon issues of labor and capital and particularly the effects of new technology. The writer for the *New York Times,* in his critique of the western formula, added the note that the "inroads of civilization always annoy the fan. No successful Westerns have been made with automobiles."[16] An interesting assessment but wholly false. The majority of series westerns are set in the modern West, or at least a West that is not historically circumscribed, and the inroads of modernity (if not "civilization") are fundamental to the form. This was no mere simplistic staging of conservative reaction to the encroachment of an alien culture; the films invoked in complex plays with and against each other such notions as rural/urban, stasis/change, and nostalgia/contemporaniety. *The Big Show* is a striking example of how social and cultural change registers in ways that complicate such binary thinking. The film does not take the Texas centennial as an opportunity for a nostalgic recalling of a lost frontier past; while the traditional skills of horsemanship and cowpunching suggest a point around which to articulate a sense of shared history, the Texans stage their centennial within ultramodern architectural spaces. The camera lingers on buildings, statuary, and sculptures of a

highly stylized, almost futuristic, modernity and establishes the public spaces of the new. Crowds of excited spectators enter into monu-
mental stadiums that create the arena for the show. This might mean
that the centennial is staged as an exhibition of nostalgia for a lost past.
But, more exactly, it is a celebration of the West that integrates both
dimensions (of modernity and of tradition) in its depiction of a culture thriving on the lived experience of historical change. Modern
buildings, massive public spaces, automobiles, radio stations, film stars,
advertising, and commercial sponsorship define the West just as much
as land, cattle, and rural tradition.

The paean to modernity that *The Big Show* projects, however, ob-
scures the real historical conditions that forced massive migration from
rural districts to towns and cities in the 1930s. The longer history of
the South and the Midwest throughout the nineteenth century is that
of its mechanization, which intensified in the years between 1900 and
1920. This was the period that witnessed the introduction of tractors
and machine-powered combines that permitted farmers to plow and
harvest great swathes of the native grasslands with less and less labor.
The new western historian Richard White asserts that the great increase
in the use of tractors came in the 1920s just as the cost of implements
and machinery on the northern plains rose by 240 percent.[17] Thus the
initial benefits of mechanization yielded reduced labor costs and more
cost-effective production but also sowed the seeds for the catastroph-
ic collapse of the farming economy in the 1930s: increased investment
in new technologies required that farmers borrow money and, to re-
pay their capital debts, to increase profits. This demanded the production of greater yields, a practice that was instrumental in stimulating
a cycle of overproduction and glut. With a saturated market, produce
prices plummeted, in turn leaving small farmers unable to discharge
their debts. In the 1930s drought, erosion, and the Great Depression
cataclysmically exacerbated the cycle of overproduction begun in the
1920s. As John Opie in *The Law of the Land* has noted, during the 1930s
more than 25 percent of all Americans still lived and worked in rural
communities, but throughout the decade "prices for farm goods
dropped to less than half between 1929 and 1932; net income fell by
70 percent." However, the "dedicated farm family hard at work on its
own land still represented an American ideal."[18] In his study of south-
western migration to California James N. Gregory complements Opie's
point when he notes that even though "steady work, either farm or non-
farm, eluded the majority [of migrants] and . . . nearly half finished

the decade earning less than a standard subsistence income . . . there are other issues to consider": "Property, even just a vacant lot upon which a house would someday stand, symbolized much of what had recently eluded them. It was the land they no longer or had never been able to own. It was the home that economic conditions back east and migratory compulsions out west tried to deny them. It was the security that they along with so many other Depression era Americans craved."[19] The social effects of changes in the commercialization of farming, then, "amounted to an invasion of a pastoral, paternalistic society by an agrarian, capitalistic society."[20] The vision of prosperity and popular engagement with consumer culture presented in *The Big Show* is a benign development of the series western's concern to depict the turmoil that rural workers and farmers faced during the 1930s. Series westerns more typically work on the terrain of dispossession and suggest the possibility of bridging the divide between the ideal of a successful farm and the reality of a failing farm, between being a landowner and being landless, between being part of a community and being cast adrift. In this the cowboy has a crucial role to play.

As Autry states in his autobiography: "I did not engage, for the most part, in such mundane activities as saving the old homestead or chasing bank bandits. While my solutions were a little less complex than those offered by FDR, and my methods a bit more direct, I played a kind of New Deal Cowboy who never hesitated to tackle many of the same problems: the dust bowl, unemployment, or the harnessing of power. This may have contributed to my popularity with the 1930s audiences."[21] Arguably, the traditions of the dime novel are useful for demonstrating how popular cultural fictions negotiate ideological reconciliation by mediating contemporary historical realities and formulaic narrative forms. Of the "working woman" dime novel genre, Michael Denning observes: "So a story to be a story had to be set in a contemporary time and knowable landscape, but its plot had to be out of the ordinary; 'everyday happenings,' according to this working woman's aesthetic, did not make a story. The story was an interruption in the present, a magical, fairy tale transformation of familiar landscapes and characters, a death and rebirth that turned the social world upside down, making proud ladies villains, and working-girls ladies."[22] The cowboy figure in the series western instantiates such reversals: capital is rehabilitated, repossessed land and property are restored to their rightful owners, shattered families are reunited, community divisions are repaired, the criminals are exposed, and unproductive land yields hitherto unrealized mineral or real-estate wealth. Indeed, these are Denning's "fairy tale" reversals, though clearly located not in the sphere of the supernatural but in the quotidian realities of the contemporary audience. In this the cowboy is the agent through which the banal, the mundane, the everyday are subject to "magical" transformation. Like the Jacksonian blackface minstrel that Dale Cockrell describes, the cowboy stands outside to observe the social consequences of factory labor. For Cockrell minstrelsy comments upon the new institutions of industrialization: "clocks, bosses, subordination, grimness, and 'wage slavery.'" Minstrelsy's "seeming accommodation" of racism, which benefited white middle-class America, carried with it an "underlying subversion" of the values of the powerful, which worked to affirm "traditional modes of understanding."[23] Both figures, the cowboy and the minstrel, mediate between the powerful and the powerless. Like the black mask, the cowboy's costume is a mechanism that conceals and promises a "reordering of the world."[24] In the broader sense, cowboy performances in the series western operate across states of stability and change.

An August 1938 review of Autry's *The Man from Music Mountain* (Republic, 1938) supports both Denning's analysis of the narrative transformation of contemporary landscapes and characters and Cockrell's concealed-yet-promised reordering of the world: "Its excellent story, diverging far from the beaten formula path, is as modern as tomorrow's newspaper, yet it retains the vitality and atmosphere of the West."[25] Advertising copy also dictated the promotion of *Tumbling Tumbleweeds* as portraying a "new and modern West . . . but quick triggered gunmen are still on the rampage."[26] The rolling text at the beginning of *Red River Valley* (Republic, 1936) supports Autry's declaration in his autobiography that he played the role of the New Deal cowboy: "Drought—the grim enemy that devastated once prosperous farm and ranch lands. Men have learned the bitter lesson of un-preparedness. Throughout stricken areas today, they are rallying forces to fight back with their only weapon—water." The text overlays images of raging rivers with their mighty torrents harnessed by the walls of huge dams, but this is not a government-sponsored documentary. Autry has brought a herd of cattle into town to be sold; while completing the deal, he hears that someone has killed a fifth "ditch rider" (watchman) and sabotaged yet another part of the dam that is being built. Despite the danger, Autry takes the job of ditch rider. The dam's completion is essential for the survival of the area's farms. Unknown to Autry and the dam's builders, the banker who is lending the money to pay the wages of the laborers is also the man behind the sabotage. By breaking the local farmers and ranchers, he can get their land cheaply and then sell at a premium when the land is finally irrigated.

When the banker withholds the loan for wages, the workers threaten to strike. To calm the rising tide of anger Autry sings "Red River Valley"—delaying the workers long enough for the wages to arrive. However, someone steals the money, and Autry is accused of the theft. The workers split into two camps—those willing to be patient just a little longer and those who intend to tear down the construction for which they have not been paid. As the two groups confront one another, the soundtrack plays Wagner's "Ride of the Valkyries." Before Autry arrives with the stolen money and reveals the true villains, the two sides engage and a bloody battle ensues. Autry's more utilitarian costume partly signals the more overt proletarian address of this film—he forsakes the elaborate shirts, pressed pants, and decorated short cowboy boots and instead wears Levi's over his boots and plain western shirts.

The film effectively ties issues arising from the dust bowl (and the New Deal's response) to labor agitation. Press reports, if not newsreel images, of violent clashes between strikers and strikebreakers had contemporary currency: violent opposition had met the 1929 Carolina Piedmont textile strikes; the 1931 coal miner strikes in Harlan and Bell counties, Kentucky; the wave of strikes across the South by miners and laundry workers; and the general strikes in San Francisco in 1934.[27] Autry's and other series westerns recognized the volatility of the relationship between labor and capital during this period. Though the films often allude to the representation of these conflicts rather than express them directly, the unfair treatment of labor by capital (often represented by villainous businessmen and bankers who sport little black moustaches) forms a core theme in many series westerns. Regardless of Red River Valley's anemic representation of labor disputes, the series western was one of the few spaces within American cinema's vast output during the 1930s that afforded any recognition whatsoever of the issue. More frequently, social antagonism was not overtly figured but present nonetheless in the form of criminal individuals and organizations.

"By 1937," writes the film scholar Charles Eckert, "the figure of the gangster had required a remarkable symbolic richness" and had, by the mid-1930s, become a stock character in series westerns. His function was clear-cut: an alien interruption of the body politic. As an emanation from the city, usually Chicago, and ethnically inscribed, generally as Italian, the gangster was doubly marked as an outsider. Eckert notes that every "personal mannerism and every artifact of his world resonated with meaning. And he had also become a *vade mecum* for anyone in search of a scapegoat."[28] Series westerns such as *Gun Smoke* (Paramount, 1931), *Crossfire* (RKO, 1933), and Autry's *The Old Corral* and *The Big Show* use the character of the gangster as an emblem of urban corruption, a salutary warning of what can transpire if society does not check the rush to embrace the new. In the context of the series western, the heroine's characterization as a consumer of nonessential goods locates her with the realm of modernity; the gangster is similarly allied to the feminine sphere of consumption through his narcissistic tendencies, fancy suits, and elegant automobiles. The feminized gangster performs a similar function to Smiley's drag act, effectively deflecting attention from the dandified cowboy hero. The sphere of the already criminalized and suitably alien figure of the gangster, then, holds the accusation of gender transgression. Just as significantly, the gangster suggests that the threat posed to the community is external—foreign and urban—so that his suppression enables a satisfying sense of narrative closure around his expulsion by the community.

More often, though, a more immediate and local character is the threat to the community; unlike the gangster, he is not so readily identifiable as a member of the criminal fraternity: sheriffs, judges, landowners, bankers, and businessmen, those who are ostensibly representatives of, or figureheads for, the community. Time and again these films show authority figures as corrupt. The mask of bourgeois respectability hides their essential dishonesty, which the films often establish through the characters' business connections to the local saloon. Indeed, saloon keepers and judges are usually one and the same person, with alcohol as the major signifier of a debased politico.

The series western poses two solutions to the corruption at the head of the community: legal and extralegal. Films such as Autry's *Guns and Guitars* and *Colorado Sunset* (Republic, 1939) vanquish the criminal fraternity through the use of the ballot box. In both scenarios Autry stands for sheriff against the puppet installed by the villains, who, in *Guns and Guitars*, use free beer to entice the voters. In both films Autry's campaigns capitalize instead upon the popularity of his singing and upon the women of the communities, who turn their admiration for Autry into votes by cajoling their menfolk into supporting his candidacy.

Tex Ritter in *Mystery of the Hooded Horseman* (Grand National, 1937) is also the people's choice in the fight against crime, but in this instance their only recourse to justice is to step outside the legitimate means of redress and form a vigilante group—the Victory Riders. Because the town of Red Eye is being terrorized by a gang of horsemen that hides behind hoods and capes embellished with Maltese crosses and skulls and crossbones, the sheriff, the legally elected representative, is powerless in his attempts to establish order—whom should he arrest? Early in the narrative the bad guys kill the co-owner of the Four-Star mine, pull back their hoods, and reveal their identities to the audience (one thug is played by Charles King, who was regularly cast as the villain in series westerns) so that only the sheriff does not know who they are. However, the film has not yet given the identity of the "Big Boss." The denouement reveals that he is the other partner in the mine who has been attempting to take control after learning that the ore is particularly valuable. "But," as the niece of his dead partner exclaims, "I don't understand. Why should he raid his own mine?" "To drive you out, Nancy," replies Tex. "See, Farley was the brains behind a big organization of thieves and cut-throats. They were trying to get control of this entire valley. They almost did." The sheriff too asks Ritter to explain what has been going on: "How did he manage to keep undercover for so long?" "Oh, that was easy," says Ritter. "See, the mine shaft connected with this hideout here. He could come and go as he pleased without being discovered." "Well," says the sheriff, "that explains everything." Well, not quite. Actually, the co-owner remained undiscovered because he appeared to be part of the community, an upstanding citizen and a victim of the hooded riders' campaign of terror. That he was in fact none of these things but instead sought to destroy the community as the brains behind the hooded riders is further testimony to the idea of the series western as a world turned upside down. At one point Ritter wears the costume of the hooded riders in order to infiltrate the gang but ends up being arrested for being a member. To sort out this mess the film calls upon the agency of the extralegal vigilante group that Tex has organized, a force strong enough to vanquish the terrorist hooded riders. In the Roy Rogers *Saga of Death Valley* (Republic, 1939) this recourse to extralegal means in order to overcome a villain who is posing as a pillar of society and an upholder of law and order leads to the call for the riders of Death Valley to join an organization that will protect them from the "protective association."

The use of hooded capes as a disguise to hide identity, whether used by the villains or, as in the Tim McCoy series for Victory Pictures—where he plays the character Lightnin' Bill Carson (otherwise known as the Phantom) in order to protect the innocent—offers strong visual parallel to the Ku Klux Klan. The series western historian Don Miller explicitly forges this connection in his reading of the Three Mesquiteers' *The Night Riders* (Republic, 1939).[29] However, in the films where the good guys don hooded robes in order to right injustice, there is no suggestion of support for the Klan, but their shared concern with using theatrical disguises and the use of extrajudicial means to right perceived wrongs nevertheless creates an uneasy symbolic relationship.

Other extralegal forces deployed in series westerns were the privately engaged detective agencies. Their costumes may have been less theatrical than those displayed by hooded night riders, but as villainous figures they must have carried an even more frightening reputation for an audience of 1930s workers. As exemplified by such agencies as the Pinkertons and Baldwin Felts, private detectives were essentially hired armies used as strikebreakers and union busters.[30] Though the series western shies away from any overt representation of these organizations as enforcers of unjust labor laws, their equivalents appear in such films as *Rainbow Valley* (Lone Star/Monogram, 1935), in which a private army of thugs holds miners captive, and in *Red River Valley*, where hoodlums beat up the men trying to build the dam. Other films, for example, *The Days of Jesse James*, portray private detectives as self-interested: the Worthington Railroad Police (stand-ins for Pinkertons) are more concerned about gaining the reward for Jesse's capture than in justice. Indeed, the film shows them to be particularly contemptible when they bomb the home of Jesse's mother, injuring her and Jesse's half-brother. The Autry film *Public Cowboy #1* (Republic, 1937) humorously holds a detective agency up for ridicule. The story concerns the use of technology by modern-day rustlers, who use shortwave radio, airplanes, and refrigerator trucks. The rustlers' scientific management of their business at first baffles the old-time sheriff. The farmers want to bring in a professional crime fighter and so hire the Quakenbush Detective Agency. When the detective arrives, leading his "army" of uniformed men in armored cars and motorcycles with sidecars, the populace cheers him, but Frog Millhouse mocks him, singing "The Defective Detective from Brooklyn." Autry discovers their whereabouts by intercepting the rustlers' radio calls and informs the detectives, who set off in pursuit, followed by the cowboys. However, the detectives get bogged down in a river, and the cowboys ride by and capture the criminals—Autry's combination of technology and down-home cunning wins the day.

Despite the prevalence of corrupt businessmen, the Republic westerns do not advocate radical solutions to the problems of the day. But they do align themselves with the ideals of Roosevelt's New Deal through their support of self-help combined with government assistance. The films often explain away lack of immediate government relief from the problems of the depression by blaming economic hardship on the local actions of selfish business interests—the sabotaging of irrigation dams—rather than point the finger at any national explanation. Often, they excuse the federal government from taking action because the issue is basically a local or state affair. This is what occurs in *Billy the Kid Returns* when a federal official demands that the marshal aid the local populace in the fight against the big ranch corporations but is told by the marshal that this is a local dispute and federal officers are powerless. This scenario removes any responsibility from a government represented as basically honest and well intentioned while justifying the use of individual and extralegal action to solve the problem.

Consequently, a number of the Republic westerns feature stories whose main theme is the smashing of trusts and monopolies. Running alongside the ranchers' terrorizing of the homesteaders in *Billy the Kid Returns* is the story of competition between store owners. Morgenson burns out the McSween store in order to gain complete control of the supply and pricing of goods. Acting as Billy the Kid, Roy Rogers defends not only the homesteaders but also the new store that has opened in Lincoln, whose motto is "The Golden Rule Sells for Less." Similarly, the Cattlemen's Protective Association in *Colorado Sunset* is a cartel designed to monopolize the local milk market. The villain spreads the rumor that a trucking company is behind the scam. Autry soon discovers the trucking company is an honest family-run firm that began more than sixty years earlier with a single wagon in the same community. The trucking company is a representative of a benign capitalism. The system itself is sound, but it needs an active and vigilant citizenship to maintain the necessary checks and balances. The central event in the film is the election of Autry as the town's sheriff—democratic participation ensures the vanquishing of the villains.

Though social and economic critiques are systemic to the 1930s series westerns, they became much more pronounced toward the end of the decade in Republic's westerns and particularly in Roy Rogers's first starring role, in *Under Western Stars* (1938). This film, alongside others such as John Wayne's penultimate Three Mesquiteers outing, *Wyoming Outlaw* (1939), is relatively hard-hitting in its commentary on the issues raised by the dust bowl and the depression and their effects on the rural population.

Under Western Stars begins with images of newspapers superimposed over film of a farm engulfed in a dust cloud: "DUST AND DROUTH SWEEP SOUTHWEST, RANCHERS ASK U.S. AID, CATTLEMEN FIGHT FOR WATER." Then the film cuts to an image of a huge dammed reservoir, where two cattlemen are engaged in a gunfight with Great Western Power and Water Company guards (another private army). Roy and Smiley intercede and open the dam's valves. The sheriff arrests them but soon turns them loose. The townspeople of Sageville are wholly on the side of the ranchers and against the company that is charging exorbitant rates. Elected to Congress, Rogers promises to cut the rates to the bone or have the federal government take control of the water supply. Unable to get the ear of influential politicians, Rogers arranges a western party at a country club. The scene begins with Rogers calling the dance and holding the attention of his esteemed audience. He then introduces the main attraction. Newsreel images of the dust bowl are projected onto a screen, and Roy begins his narration, individualizing the stories of the farmers and ranchers. He then latches onto the tune that the band has been quietly and gently playing and sings "Dust."

Frankie Marvin and Gene Autry wrote "Dust" especially for the picture. It is an extraordinary song, easily equal to any written by the great dust bowl balladeer Woody Guthrie. Its theme is paradise turned to hell. Over a slow marching rhythm the song tells of the coming of the dust bowl:

> Dust, dust, dust in the skies,
> Dust on the trail and dust in my eyes.
> Dust, dust, can't see the sun,
> Can't find my way, the dust has won.

In the chorus Rogers makes a hopeless appeal to God to relieve the suffering: "Oh, Lord please ease my pain—Oh, Lord where is your rain / and sunshine." At the bridge the song excerpts the tune and a few lines from "Home on the Range." Used with intended irony (the newsreel images have cut to scenes of fertile farmland and roaming cattle), the section concludes with "what has become of the range?" The song provides no answer, only the belief that the dust bowl augurs eternity. Both Autry and Rogers recorded the song for record release; the former's version moves at a faster clip, leaves out "Home on the Range," and instead repeats a verse. Autry had the hit, but Rogers's version is the more emotive.

Rogers's performance wins over the politicians who decide to tour his state to see for themselves the plight of the ranchers. However, Rogers has used newsreel images of the dust bowl filmed in another state; when the members of Congress arrive in Sageville and discover this, they refuse to support the bill for federal control of the dam. Nevertheless, in the same way that the film is self-reflexive in its use of film as an able persuader of public opinion and of the power of the singing cowboy's performance to engage an audience, Rogers again sets up a complex masquerade to win back the politicians. As in the series western's use of disguise, this film uses illusion to reveal a reality. As the members of Congress and their entourage are driving to the dam, "bandits" (cowboy impostors) hold them up and swap their horses for the cars. The party, which has not brought water along, attempts to ride back to Sageville. The politicians and aides hear the sound of singing and find Rogers and Smiley camped for the night. The group is by now desperate for water, but our two heroes have only enough for the women. Come morning, the group rides in search of water, and Rogers leads a tour of the drought-ravaged land. Appropriately, a dust storm blows up, and the politicians are finally persuaded to back Rogers's bill, even after they learn that the whole setup has been an elaborate ruse. Meanwhile, the ranchers, who are unaware of the changed events, have decided to take matters into their own hands and blow up the dam, which will lose them the newly won government support. Following a mad dash, Rogers manages to climb aboard a careening wagon loaded with dynamite and turn it into a ravine, where it harmlessly explodes.

The film exposes greedy and exploitive capitalists who put their profits above the common good, and it sanctions federal control of a particular public utility. It argues that for government to become involved in what are apparently local issues, it needs to become conscious of the effects of big business on small consumers. The film shows the politicians to be both geographically and socially distant from those affected by environmental catastrophe, until Rogers arrives in Washington. But when he provides the necessary evidence, they are willing to take action. The film also argues that violent independent action will ensure that the government does not favor the small businessman.

In *Saga of Death Valley* cowboys sing "Bury Me Not on the Lone Prairie," a song that a character comments gives her "the creeps." "It reminds me," she says, "that everything is wrong in this old world and nothing is right." The audience for Republic's westerns were men, women, and children from small-town, rural, and urban neighborhoods, working-class families that were habitual consumers of cinema and that wanted what Denning calls a "magical, fairy tale transformation of familiar landscapes and characters," where everything that is wrong is turned right. This is precisely the world that series and singing westerns envisioned.

CONCLUSION

History may yet record, as Gene Autry's brightest achievement the reinstatement of the Western . . . back on the screens of the United States for other purposes than to bring the kids in on a Saturday matinee.

—*Exhibitor,* November 29, 1939

Last summer he [Joe Pasternak, producer of *Destry Rides Again*] looked at Gene Autry's fan mail and took heed.

—*Picture Play,* February 1940

The U.S. people are going to the movies more than they ever did before. . . . In many a defense center theaters were on a 24-hour day, to accommodate swing shifters. . . . Theater managers found audiences the rowdiest in their memory: they howled, hissed and booed at pictures, demanded Westerns, carved their initials on seats, sometimes even fired buckshot at the screen. War workers brought alarm clocks, set them to go off when they had to leave for work.

—*Time,* March 15, 1943

It would be too much to claim that the success of Autry's films led the major studios to emphatically return to the production of prestige westerns in 1939, as exemplified by *Destry Rides Again, Stagecoach, Dodge City, Jesse James, Oklahoma Kid, Union Pacific,* and *Let Freedom Ring.* The reasons were far more complex. On one level, the studios needed to placate independent exhibitors, whose continued complaints against blind and block booking had led the government to renewed action against the industry's monopolistic practices. Furthermore, testimony about proposed antitrust legislation cited Hollywood's self-censoring Production Code as a political apparatus that excluded the production of films seeking to deal with social and political issues. Hollywood, some observers suggested, not only held a monopoly on production, distribution, and exhibition but also had control of the expression of ideas. By producing high-class westerns, Hollywood hoped to play to both first-run houses and the independent sector. As an allegorical story form, the western proved to be politically expedient in allowing for the introduction of controversial issues without their explicit engagement. Hollywood conceived the westerns as historical stories that addressed contemporary concerns, but they were sufficiently ambiguous to avoid accusations that the industry favored any particular domestic political factions, such as the isolationists or interventionists.

The continuing popularity of the series western and the deepening of Autry's appeal to the independent sector and its audiences helped consolidate the major studios' understanding of the genre. This was a genre that, if exploited as an exceptional *American* art form and given the casting and production values of a prestige picture, could appeal across class, gender, generation, and political divisions. Autry's success with a female audience may also have suggested that it was possible to cast, apparently against type, matinee idols such as Tyrone Power and Robert Taylor in westerns—that the form did not necessitate the casting of more elemental actors, as exemplified by the likes of Gary Cooper. However, Autry's success with both male and female patrons probably did not register with the production heads of the major studios until after the first cycle of prestige westerns in 1939. When Autry crossed over from the *Motion Picture Herald*'s top ten poll of western stars in 1940 to appear fourth (behind Mickey Rooney, Spencer Tracy, and Clark Gable) in the poll of the nation's top box-office draws, he took the industry totally by surprise, at least on the evidence of the event's coverage in the fan magazines.

In fan magazines such as *Motion Picture, Picture Play*, and *Screenland*, writers struggled to explain Autry's appeal, recycling the claim of Republic Pictures that Autry averaged 12,000 pieces of fan mail per week and a record 50,103 letters in one unspecified month—figures that eclipsed the mail received by Clark Gable, who topped the *Motion Picture Herald*'s poll. The writers emphasized Autry's "outsider" status; although he lived in Hollywood, he somehow remained divorced from its social whirl and shenanigans. Photo spreads took the reader into the Autry household, where the homey emphasis reinforced the representation of Autry as a domesticated cowboy—the home was both ranch house and idyllic suburban domicile. The fan magazines used Autry's eight-year marriage to Ina Mae, who came from a small town in Oklahoma, to exemplify the new star's virtuous down-home life style, a further contrast to the love lives of Hollywood's more celebrated citizens. The words that these publications most commonly used to explain Autry's appeal were *simplicity, sincerity,* and *warmth*—adjectives unlike any they used to describe Gable. This national recognition was unprecedented in Autry's career. Until this point the fan magazines had virtually ignored not only him but also all the other series western stars. The major metropolitan newspapers had also paid scant attention. The *New York Times* had offered coverage on only two occasions during the 1930s, the first in 1938 when Autry had gone on "strike" and the second in August 1939 when Bosley Crowther introduced him to readers as a "cowboy without a lament." "Are you not acquainted with Gene?" asks Crowther; the twelve column inches that follow then replay the facts of his career.[1]

National recognition came in a different form in 1940 when Wrigley's chewing gum became the sponsor of Autry's new weekly network radio show, *Melody Ranch,* on CBS. By this time Autry's solo appeal was felt to be broad enough to carry a network show. Rather than appearing as part of the show, as happened with the *National Barn Dance,* Autry was now the undisputed star—the main attraction. The half-hour program, which ran for sixteen years, featured musical performances and a fifteen-minute western drama. Even more than his position in the *Motion Picture Herald*'s poll and the subsequent press coverage, *Melody Ranch* confirmed that the singing cowboy had shifted from the margins of American culture to its center.

A six-week personal appearance tour of the British Isles and the Irish Free State during August and September 1939 confirmed Autry's international standing. "At noon today a tall young man [Autry was neither particularly tall nor young] with a Max Miller smile under a ten-gallon hat will ride his horse into the ballroom of the Savoy Hotel in the Strand. The name is Gene Autry and he is the world's most popular screen cowboy," one paper told its readers.[2] All the English daily newspapers reported the lunch of Autry and his horse Champion at the Savoy, many noting that in Britain alone Autry's pictures had sold more than 172 million tickets. This extraordinary statistic gained some credence from the tumultuous reception that he received from fans both in London and in cities such as Manchester, Birmingham, Cardiff, Leeds, and Newcastle. In Glasgow alone 50,000 turned out to greet Autry, which, according to one newspaper "set-up an all-time record for public demonstrations of popularity" in the city.[3] Fans packed theaters and the surrounding streets on a scale not witnessed during promotional tours by other Hollywood stars. But Autry's reception in Dublin eclipsed that by British fans; police estimates suggested that 500,000 to 750,000 people joined in the parade through the city's streets. It was the largest crowd in Dublin's history.

Peer recognition arrived in the form of an invitation by the American Society of Composers, Authors and Publishers for Autry to appear at the Music Hall at New York World's Fair, on Thursday, October 24, 1940. This was to be a showcase to celebrate U.S. composers. Beginning with "The Star-Spangled Banner," the show proceeded through the highlights of American symphonies and then progressed to a selection of

Gene Autry (beneath the banner on the left) surrounded by the crowd that greeted him on his first visit to Dublin, Ireland, 1939. (Photos provided courtesy of the Autry Qualified Interest Trust and the Autry Foundation. © 2001 by the Autry Qualified Interest Trust and the Autry Foundation.)

popular songs —"Happy Days Are Here Again," "Santa Claus Is Coming to Town," "When the Blue of the Night Meets the Gold of the Day"—which was capped by an appearance of the octogenarian Harry Von Tilzer, composer of "Only a Bird in a Gilded Cage." Billy Hill offered "The Last Round-Up," W. C. Handy presented "St. Louis Blues," Jules Bledsoe of *Showboat* fame performed "Ol' Man River," Richard Rodgers and Lorenz Hart performed two numbers, Johnny Green presented "Body and Soul," and Jerome Kern on piano accompanied a Gershwin tribute. And Gene Autry filled the penultimate spot, bowing out to no less a personage than Irving Berlin and his "God Bless America."[4]

Autry would have other successes in the years that followed but none, I think, were as culturally significant. The figure of the singing

Gene Autry (*left*), Irving Berlin, Richard Rodgers, and Jerome Kern at the Music Hall, New York World's Fair, 1940. (Photos provided courtesy of the Autry Qualified Interest Trust and the Autry Foundation. © 2001 by the Autry Qualified Interest Trust and the Autry Foundation.)

cowboy had changed from being a nascent theatrical masquerade for aspiring musicians hoping to carve out a recording and radio career in the late 1920s to an important part of multimillion-dollar media industries. The cowboy became the figure that confirmed the respectability and commercial viability of the burgeoning musical genre that would become known as country and western. Autry, in particular, but also its other series western stars, gave Republic Pictures the financial base from which it hoped to become a major competitor with the other Hollywood studios.

The singing cowboys appealed to a diverse yet limited audience. The films introduced specific attractions for particular sections of that audience, though the filmmakers made sure that these did not have the undesired effect of alienating other patrons. The emphasis on music and comedy developed in Autry's films in particular had cross-generational, cross-gender appeal. But during the 1930s the films' address to a working-class audience circumscribed this solicitation. The films appealed to this audience by emphasizing specific story themes that were either covertly or overtly concerned with the struggle between labor and capital. They further compounded this class-specific address by drawing upon performance traditions that spoke directly to the films' constituency.

As the nation's economic situation improved, and dislocated southern and midwestern migrants formed, for example, a significant part of the core workforce in the rapidly expanding armament industries, the series western's concern with their plight diminished, as did the films' engagement with rural social issues. After World War II these demographic shifts and a more widely spread affluence help explain the major studios' postwar commitment to the production of westerns, which lasted until the end of the 1950s. The major studios now catered to the tastes of the newly moneyed and recently established urban audience that had previously formed the core constituency for the 1930s series westerns. The continued popularity of the genre suggested that this audience had not lost its taste for western adventures and romance but no longer felt the same fears around dispossession, displacement, and economic insecurity of the depression years. The postwar westerns addressed a different set of anxieties and desires—and that is another story.

Going to leave this country, sure going to leave it soon
And this old world sure going to have my room.
When I leave here, just hang crepe upon the door
I won't be dead, just won't be here no more.

—Frank Hutchison, "Worried Blues"

NOTES

INTRODUCTION

1. "Gene Autry," *Daily Telegraph* (London), Oct. 5, 1998, p. 23.
2. W. J. Weatherby, "Gene Autry: The Singing Cowboy," *Guardian* (London), Oct. 3, 1998, p. 22.
3. *Republic Reporter* (London), Oct. 1, 1939, n.p., private collection of Alex Gordon.
4. Weatherby, "Gene Autry."

CHAPTER ONE: BY THE COSTUME WE MAY TELL THE MAN

1. Thomas Beer, *The Mauve Decade: American Life at the End of the Nineteenth Century* (London: Alfred A. Knopf, 1926), 66.
2. Christopher Benfey, *The Double Life of Stephen Crane: A Biography* (London: Vintage, 1994), 8.
3. Daryl Jones, *The Dime Novel Western* (Bowling Green, Ohio: Popular Press/Bowling Green State University, 1978), 106.
4. Richard Slotkin, *Gunfighter Nation: The Myth of the Frontier in Twentieth-Century America* (New York: HarperCollins, 1993), 127.
5. Michael Denning, *Mechanic Accents: Dime Novels and Working-Class Culture in America* (London: Verso, 1987), 163.
6. Ibid., 160.
7. Ibid., 157.
8. Marcus Klein, *Easterns, Westerns, and Private Eyes: American Matters, 1870–1900* (Madison: University of Wisconsin Press, 1994), 67–130.
9. Richard Ohmann, *Selling Culture: Magazines, Markets, and Class at the Turn of the Century* (London: Verso, 1996).
10. Ibid., 331.

11. Ibid., 336.

12. Ibid., 337.

13. Theodore Roosevelt, *Ranch Life and the Hunting Trail* (1896; rpt., Gloucester, U.K.: Alan Sutton, 1985), 6.

14. Ibid., 53.

15. Ibid., 85.

16. Ibid., 54.

17. Ibid., 11.

18. Ibid., 7.

19. Slotkin, *Gunfighter Nation,* 29–62. In addition to Slotkin's work on the connection between Turner's thesis and the writings of Roosevelt, Wister, and Remington, see Edward G. White, *The Eastern Establishment and the Eastern Experience: The West of Fredric Remington, Theodore Roosevelt, and Owen Wister* (New Haven, Conn.: Yale University Press, 1968); Gerald D. Nash, *Creating the West: Historical Interpretations, 1890–1990* (Albuquerque: University of New Mexico Press, 1991). See also Ann Fabian, "History for the Masses: Commercializing the Western Past," in *Under an Open Sky: Rethinking America's Western Past,* ed. William Cronon, George Miles, and Jay Gitlin (New York: W. W. Norton, 1992), 223–38.

20. Emerson Hough, *The Story of the Cowboy* (1897; rpt., New York: D. Appleton, 1912), viii.

21. Ibid., 2.

22. Ibid., 238.

23. Ibid., 51.

24. Ibid., 33.

25. Owen Wister, "The Evolution of the Cow-Puncher" (1895), reprinted in Ben Merchant Vorpahl, *My Dear Wister: The Frederic Remington–Owen Wister Letters* (Palo Alto, Calif.: American West, 1972), 80.

26. Ibid.

27. Ibid.

28. Ibid.

29. Ibid., 81.

30. Ibid., 41–43.

31. Slotkin, *Gunfighter Nation,* 181.

32. Frank Norris, *Novels and Essays* (New York: Library of America, 1986), 1179.

33. Ibid., 586–87. Norris wrote a number of short western stories featuring cowboys. Some of these are collected in Frank Norris, *A Deal in Wheat and Other Stories of the Old and New West* (New York: Doubleday, Page, 1903), including "A Memorandum of Sudden Death," which was inspired by a Remington painting. Norris composed the story as if it were a journal that had been written by one of the dead soldiers.

34. Richard Maxwell Brown, *No Duty to Retreat: Violence and Values in American History and Society* (Norman: University of Oklahoma Press, 1991), 87–128.

35. Norris, *Novels and Essays,* 1179.

36. Ibid., 1176.

37. Ibid., 781.

38. Ibid., 564. This construction of the character of Marcus is carried through in *Greed*, the film adaptation of *McTeague* (MGM, 1924). Marcus wears a fancy shirt, in strong contrast to the gray or dark shirts of the other cowboys. He looks foolish; they do not.

39. Ibid., 542.

40. Stephen Crane, *Prose and Poetry* (New York: Library of America, 1984), 809.

41. Zeese Papanikolas, *Trickster in the Land of Dreams* (Lincoln: University of Nebraska Press, 1995), 73–74.

42. James Cape, "From Black Slave to Texas Cowboy," in *Looking Far West: The Search for the American West in History, Myth and Literature*, ed. Frank Bergon and Zeese Papanikolas (New York: New American Library, 1978), 280–82.

43. Nat Love, *The Life and Adventures of Nat Love* (1907; rpt., Lincoln: University of Nebraska Press, 1995), 156–57.

44. Jones, *Dime Novel Western*, 87.

45. Jane Tompkins, *West of Everything: The Inner Life of Westerns* (London: Oxford University Press, 1992), 39–40.

46. See also Judy Alter and A. T. Row, eds., *Unbridled Spirits: Short Fiction about Women in the Old West* (Ft. Worth: Texas Christian University Press, 1994). A useful collection but, bizarrely, does not include Bower.

47. Klein, *Easterns, Westerns, and Private Eyes*, 101.

48. Denning, *Mechanic Accents*, 193–94.

49. Mary Clearman Blew, introduction to B. M. Bower, *Chip of the Flying U* (1904; rpt., Lincoln: University of Nebraska Press, 1995), 8.

50. Bower, *Chip of the Flying U*, 246.

51. B. M. Bower, *The Happy Family of the Flying U* (1910; rpt., Lincoln: University of Nebraska Press, 1996), 219–20.

52. B. M. Bower, *Lonesome Land* (1912; rpt., Lincoln: University of Nebraska Press, 1997), 287–88.

53. Ibid., vi.

54. Beer, *Mauve Decade*, 236–37.

55. Owen Wister, *The Virginian* (1902; rpt., Oxford: Oxford University Press, 1998), 11–13. This edition also includes "The Evolution of the Cow-Puncher" and an excellent introduction by Robert Shulman.

56. Wister, "Evolution of the Cow-Puncher," 86.

57. Crane, "Twelve O'Clock," in *Prose and Poetry*, 830.

58. Edward T. LeBlanc, ed., *Denver Dan and the Road Agents* and *Buffalo Bill's Tomahawk Duel* (Derby, Conn.: Gold Star, 1964), 82.

59. Jones, *Dime Novel Western*, 109–10.

60. B. M. Bower, "On with the Dance," in *My Best Western Story: A Collection of Stories Chosen by Their Own Authors* (London: Faber and Faber, 1935), 9.

61. Quoted in Anders Breidlid, Frederik C. Brogger, Oyvind T. Gulliksen, and Torbjorn Sirevag, eds., *American Culture: An Anthology of Civilisation Texts* (London: Routledge, 1995), 39.

CHAPTER TWO: LIBERTY'S CUCKOOS

1. Dust jacket blurb for Lee Clark Mitchell, *Westerns: Making the Man in Fiction and Film* (Chicago: University of Chicago Press, 1997).

2. Richard Slotkin, *Gunfighter Nation: The Myth of the Frontier in Twentieth-Century America* (New York: HarperCollins, 1993), 169.

3. Owen Wister, "The Evolution of the Cow-Puncher," *Harper's Monthly*, Sept. 1895, pp. 602–17, reprinted in *Owen Wister's West: Selected Articles*, ed. Robert Murray Davis (Albuquerque: University of New Mexico Press, 1987), 33–53.

4. Steven J. Ross, *Working-Class Hollywood: Silent Film and the Shaping of Class in America* (Princeton, N.J.: Princeton University Press, 1998), 42.

5. Ibid., 68–69.

6. Though an intertitle gives the location as Coney Island, the scenes were actually shot in a Los Angeles park.

7. For more on the figure of the rube in early cinema, see Charles Musser, *Before the Nickelodeon: Edwin S. Porter and the Edison Manufacturing Company* (Berkeley: University of California Press, 1991), 165.

8. See Robert Anderson, "The Role of the Western Film Genre in Industry Competition, 1907–11," *Journal of the University Film Association* 31:2 (Spring 1979): 19–26.

9. Mitchell has convincingly argued that the most popular western novel of the 1910s, Zane Grey's *Riders of the Purple Sage* (1912), is a staging of the white slave narrative (*Westerns,* 120–49). Much could also be made of this narrative conceit in the early film western, but despite a growing library on film and white slavery, particularly *Traffic in Souls* (1913), white slavery and the film western remains untouched. See, for example, Janet Staiger, *Bad Women: Regulating Sexuality in Early American Cinema* (Minneapolis: University of Minnesota Press, 1995); Tom Gunning, "From Kaleidoscope to the X-Ray: Urban Spectatorship, Poe, Benjamin, and *Traffic in Souls,*" *Wide Angle* 19:4 (1999): 25–61; Shelly Stamp Lindsey, "Is Any Girl Safe?: Female Spectators at the White Slave Films," *Screen* 37:1 (1996): 1–15; Lee Grieveson, "Policing the Cinema: *Traffic in Souls* at Ellis Island," *Screen* 38:2 (1997): 149–71.

Another example of the western's direct engagement with contemporary political issues occurs in the "frontier comedy," *When Roaring Gulch Got Suffrage* (Universal, date unknown), the poster for which was reproduced on the cover of Kay Sloan's study of the social problem film, *The Loud Silents: Origins of the Social Problem Film* (Urbana: University of Illinois Press, 1988).

10. For a more complete discussion of the city slicker, see Peter Stanfield, "The Western, 1909–14: A Cast of Villains," *Film History* 1:2 (1987): 97–112. For a more developed account of this character and his relationship to money, land, and the law, see Virginia Wright Wexman, "The Family on the Land: Race and Nationhood in Silent Westerns" in *The Birth of Whiteness: Race and the Emergence of U.S. Cinema,* ed. Daniel Bernardi (New Brunswick, N.J.: Rutgers University Press, 1996), 129–69.

11. For an analysis of medievalism and turn-of-the century U.S. culture, see T. J. Jackson Lears, *No Place of Grace: Antimodernism and the Transformation of American Culture, 1880–1920* (New York: Pantheon, 1981).

12. This idea is drawn from David R. Roediger, *The Wages of Whiteness: Race and the Making of the American Working Class* (London: Verso, 1991), and Alexander Saxton, *The Rise and Fall of the White Republic: Class Politics and Mass Culture in 19th Century America* (London: Verso, 1990).

13. *Frederic Remington, Selected Letters,* ed. Allen Splite and Marilyn Splite (New York: Abbeville, 1988), 171.

14. Richard Abel, *The Red Rooster Scare: Making Cinema American, 1900–1910* (Berkeley: University of California Press, 1999), 172.

15. Eileen Bowser, *The Transformation of Cinema, 1907–15* (New York: Charles Scribner's, 1990), 103–77.

16. Richard Ohmann, *Selling Culture: Magazines, Markets, and Class at the Turn of the Century* (London: Verso, 1996), 333–34.

17. Ibid., 334.

18. Charles M. Russell, *Word Painter: Letters, 1887–1926,* ed. Brian W. Dippie (Ft. Worth, Tex.: Amon Carter Museum, 1993), 53.

19. In particular see George N. Fenin and William K. Everson, *The Western: From Silents to the Seventies* (Harmondsworth, U.K.: Penguin, 1977), 75–108.

20. Buck Rainey, *Saddle Aces of the Cinema* (New York: A. S. Barnes, 1980), 59–82.

21. Notes on their earnings can be found in Richard Koszarski, *An Evening's Entertainment: The Age of the Silent Feature Picture, 1915–1928* (Berkeley: University of California Press, 1990), 114, 116, 279, 281.

22. Ibid., 183.

23. Ibid., 116, 183.

24. Press book for *Fighting Courage,* Ken Maynard Collection, Autry Museum of Western Heritage, Los Angeles.

25. *Exhibitors Trade Review,* July 11, 1925.

26. Press book for *The Land Beyond the Law,* Maynard Collection.

27. Ibid., and press book for *King of the Arena* (Universal, 1933), Maynard Collection.

28. Press book for *Fighting Courage.*

CHAPTER THREE: MONODIES FOR THE COWPUNCHER

1. Gilbert Seldes, *The Seven Lively Arts* (1924; rpt., New York: Sagamore, 1957), 78.

2. John A. Lomax and Alan Lomax, *Cowboy Songs and Other Frontier Ballads* (New York: Collier/Macmillan, 1986), xi.

3. John O. West, "Jack Thorp and John Lomax: Oral or Written Transmission?," *Western Folklore* 26 (1967): 113–18.

4. Nolan Porterfield, *The Last Cavalier: The Life and Times of John A. Lomax* (Urbana: University of Illinois Press, 1996), 153.

5. Ibid., 60.

6. Wister is quoted in Ben Merchant Vorpahl, *My Dear Wister: The Frederic Remington–Owen Wister Letters* (Palo Alto, Calif.: American West, 1972), 93.

7. John I. White, *Git Along Little Dogies: Songs and Songmakers of the American*

West (Urbana: University of Illinois Press, 1989). For an alternative history of cowboy songs that also contains an excellent bibliography, see Guy Logsdon, *The Whorehouse Bells Were Ringing and Other Songs Cowboys Sing* (Urbana: University of Illinois Press, 1989).

8. White, *Git Along Little Dogies,* 153–66.

9. Ibid., 63.

10. Mary M. North, *A Prairie-Schooner: A Romance of the Plains of Kansas* (Washington, D.C.: Neale, 1902), 49–51. North included five verses of "The Lost Trail."

11. Gene Bluestein, *Poplore: Folk and Pop in American Culture* (Amherst: University of Massachusetts Press, 1994), 66, 84.

12. Andy Adams, *The Log of a Cowboy: A Narrative of the Old Trail Days* (1903; rpt., New York: Airmont, 1969).

13. Ibid., 141.

14. Owen Wister, *The Virginian: A Horseman of the Plains* (1902; rpt., Oxford: Oxford University Press, 1998), 144.

15. Emerson Hough, *The Story of the Cowboy* (1897; rpt., New York: D. Appleton, 1912), 192.

16. Ibid., 142–43.

17. Janet Brown, "The Coon-Singer and the Coon-Song: A Case Study of the Performer-Character Relationship," *Journal of American Culture* 7, no. 1/2 (Spring–Summer 1984), 1–8; James H. Dormon, "Reshaping the Popular Image of Post-Reconstruction American Blacks: The 'Coon Song' Phenomenon of the Guilded Age," *American Quarterly* 40, no. 4 (1988), 440–77; Charles Hamm, *Yesterdays: Popular Song in America* (New York: Norton, 1983), 271.

18. B. M. Bower, *Chip of the Flying U* (1904; rpt., Lincoln: University of Nebraska Press, 1995), 15, 197.

19. B. M. Bower, *The Happy Family of the Flying U* (1910; rpt., Lincoln: University of Nebraska Press, 1996), 18.

20. Carson's first sessions can be heard on *Complete Recorded Works in Chronological Order,* vol. 1 (Document Records, DOCD-8014, 1997). See Gene Wiggins, *Fiddlin' Georgia Crazy: Fiddlin' John Carson, His Real World, and the World of His Songs* (Urbana: University of Illinois Press, 1987).

21. Richard A. Peterson, *Creating Country Music: Fabricating Authenticity* (Chicago: University of Chicago Press, 1997), 33.

22. Robert Cantwell, *Bluegrass Breakdown: The Making of the Old Southern Sound* (New York: Da Capo, 1992), 192.

23. Peterson, *Creating Country Music,* 40.

24. Seldes, *Seven Lively Arts,* 66.

25. Sigmund Spaeth, *Read 'Em and Weep: The Songs You Forgot to Remember* (1926; rpt., New York: Doubleday, Doran, 1935); Sigmund Spaeth, *Weep Some More, My Lady* (New York: Doubleday, Page, 1927).

26. John Tasker Howard, *Our American Music: Three Hundred Years of It* (1929; rpt., New York: Thomas Y. Crowell, 1954). Frank Shay, *My Pious Friends and Drunken Companions* (1927) and *More Pious Friends and Drunken Companions* (1928) (rpt., New York: Dover, 1961); James J. Geller, *Famous Songs and Their Stories* (New York: Macaulay, 1931).

27. Helen L. Kaufmann, *From Jehovah to Jazz: Music in America from Psalmody to the Present Day* (New York: Dodd, Mead, 1937).

28. Guy B. Johnson, *John Henry: Tracking Down a Negro Legend* (Chapel Hill: University of North Carolina Press, 1929); Newman I. White, *American Negro Folk-Songs* (Cambridge, Mass.: Harvard University Press, 1928).

29. John A. Lomax, *Songs of the Cattle Trail and Cow Camp* (New York: Macmillan, 1919); John A. Lomax and Alan Lomax, *American Folk Songs and Ballads* (New York: Macmillan, 1934).

30. Carl Sandburg, *The American Songbag* (1927; rpt., New York: Harcourt Brace Jovanovich, 1990).

31. Sigmund Spaeth, *A History of Popular Music in America* (New York: Random House, 1948), 415.

32. Cantwell, *Bluegrass Breakdown*, 34.

33. Ibid.

34. Both songs are collected on *When I Was a Cowboy: Early American Songs of the West*, vols. 1 and 2 (Yazoo, 2022 and 2023, 1996).

35. "Tom Sherman's Barroom" on *When I Was a Cowboy*. Further recordings by "authentic cowboys" can be found on *Let 'Er Buck! 25 Authentic Cowboy Songs* (Charly, CDGR 267, 1999).

36. As recorded by Taylor's Kentucky Boys on *When I Was a Cowboy*, vol. 1. Fiddlin' John Carson also recorded a version of "Dixie Cowboy" on *Complete Recorded Works in Chronological Order.* Carl Sprague recorded a version under its more famous title, "When the Work's All Done This Fall," on *Western Cowboy Ballads and Songs, 1925–1939* (Frémeaux and Associés, FA 034, 1995).

37. Wade Mainer recorded "If I Could Hear My Mother Pray Again" in 1936; it appears with thirteen like-minded odes to Mom on *Sacred Songs of Mother and Home* (Old Homestead Records, OCHS-135, 1971).

38. Moderwell is quoted in Kaufmann, *From Jehovah to Jazz*, 244.

39. The commentator is quoted in H. O. Brunn, *The Story of the Original Dixieland Jazz Band* (London: Jazz Book Club, 1963), 108.

40. Hear "Livery Stable Blues" and other earsplitting numbers on *The 75th Anniversary* (BMG, RCA Bluebird, ND90650, 1992).

41. Nick LaRocca is quoted in Brunn, *Story of the Original Dixieland Jazz Band*, 135.

42. Cantwell, *Bluegrass Breakdown*, 141.

43. Brunn, *Story of the Original Dixieland Jazz Band*, 136.

44. Ibid., 173.

45. Peterson, *Creating Country Music*, 59–62.

46. Charles Wolfe, *The Devil's Box: Masters of Southern Fiddling* (Nashville, Tenn.: Country Music Foundation Press/Vanderbilt University Press, 1997), xix.

47. These recording sessions are collected on *The Bristol Sessions* (Country Music Foundation Records, CMF-011-D, 1991), notes by Charles Wolfe.

48. *Webster's New International Dictionary* (Springfield, Mass.: G. and C. Merriam, 1932).

49. The complete recorded works of Jimmie Rodgers are collected on *The Singing Brakeman* (Bear Family Records, BCD 15540 FI, 1992).

50. David Schiff, *Gershwin: Rhapsody in Blue* (Cambridge: Cambridge Music Handbooks/Cambridge University Press, 1997), 56. Emphasis added.

51. For an account of minstrelsy and jazz see Berndt Ostendorf, "Minstrelsy and Early Jazz," *Massachusetts Review* 20 (Autumn 1979): 574–602.

52. Davis is quoted in the booklet that accompanies his *Nobody's Darlin' But Mine* (Bear Family Records, BCD 15943 E1, 1998), 5.

53. The beautifully packaged Dock Boggs, *Country Blues* (Revenant, 205, 1998), includes transcriptions of the lyrics.

54. Russell Sanjek and David Sanjek, *American Popular Music Business in the 20th Century* (Oxford: Oxford University Press, 1991), 24.

55. These two songs can be heard on Gene Autry's *Blues Singer, 1929–31: "Booger Rooger Saturday Nite!"* (Columbia Legacy, Blues 'n' Roots, CK 64987, 1997). Other significant collections of Autry from his "Jimmie Rodgers" period are the German CDs *Yodeling Gene Autry: The Life of Jimmie Rodgers* (Bronco Buster, CD 9017, 1999) and *The Early Yodeling Days of Gene Autry* (Cattle, CCD 242, 2001).

56. See Peterson, *Creating Country Music*, 86.

57. Humphries is quoted in the notes accompanying Cliff Carlisle's *Blues Yodeler and Steel Guitar Wizard* (Arhoolie, CD 7039, 1996).

58. Greil Marcus, *Mystery Train: Images of America in Rock 'n' Roll Music*, 4th rev. ed. (New York: Plume, 1997), 143.

59. Frank Norris, *Novels and Essays* (New York: Library of America, 1986), 332.

60. Ibid., 335.

61. Ibid., 337.

62. Karen Linn, *That Half-Barbaric Twang: The Banjo in American Popular Culture* (Urbana: University of Illinois Press, 1994), 25.

63. Watson's recording can be heard on *American Yodeling, 1911–1946* (Trikont US-0246-2, 1998).

64. Nick Tosches, *Country: The Twisted Roots of Rock 'n' Roll*, 3d ed. (New York: Da Capo, 1996), 249. This is the finest introduction to prewar country music. In its various editions it has been my guidebook to the heart of American music; like Jimmie Rodgers, it is peerless.

65. Ibid., 239–40.

66. Ibid., 249. Miller's Okeh sides are collected on *The Minstrel Man from Georgia* (Columbia Legacy, 483584 2, 1996). His final 1936 session is collected on *Blue Yodelers with Red Hot Accompanists* (Retrieval, RTR 79020, 1999), which also compiles Jimmie Rodgers's "jazz" sides and the novelty yodeler Roy Evans's 1928–31 sessions.

67. "Slu-Foot Lou" and "Stay away from My Chicken House" are on Autry's *Blues Singer.* Despite this aural minstrelsy, there is no evidence that Autry ever appeared in blackface makeup. According to Douglas B. Green, Autry "did blackface comedy" (Green, "The Singing Cowboy: An American Dream," in Packy Smith and Ed Hulse, eds., *Don Miller's Hollywood Corral: A Comprehensive B-Western Roundup* [Burbank, Calif.: Riverwood Press, 1993), 336]. But this is only a supposition based on Autry's youthful experience with a medicine show, one that I argue elsewhere in this book was greatly embellished and probably fabricated by his publicity agent.

68. Frank Hutchison's recordings are collected on *Complete Works in Chro-*

nological Order, 1926–29, vol. 1 (Document, DOCD-8003, 1997) with sleeve notes by Tony Russell, and *Old-Time Music from West Virginia* (Document Records, DOCD-8004, 1997). The picture of Hutchison as a cowboy is reproduced on the sleeve of his *The Train That Carried My Girl from Town* (Rounder Records, 1007, 1976).

69. Cantwell, *Bluegrass Breakdown*, 277.

70. Colin Escott, *Hank Williams: The Biography* (New York: Little Brown, 1994), 56.

71. James F. Evans, *Prairie Farmer and WLS: The Burridge D. Butler Years* (Urbana: University of Illinois Press, 1969).

72. Michele Hilmes, *Hollywood and Broadcasting: From Radio to Cable* (Urbana: University of Illinois Press, 1990), 2.

73. Ibid., 51.

74. Carrie Rodgers, *My Husband, Jimmie Rodgers* (1935; rpt., Nashville: Country Music Foundation, 1995), 146–47.

75. Gene Fowler and Bill Crawford, *Border Radio* (New York: Limelight Edition, 1990).

76. *Variety*, Dec. 11, 1934, pp. 1, 52.

77. Charles Wolfe, "The Triumph of the Hills: Country Radio, 1920–50," in *Country: The Music and the Musicians*, ed. Paul Kingsbury, Alan Axelrod, and Susan Costello (New York: Country Music Foundation/Abbeville, 1994), 51.

78. *Variety*, Dec. 11, 1934, pp. 1, 52.

79. Ibid., 52.

80. Cantwell, *Bluegrass Breakdown*, 254.

81. W. T. Lhamon Jr., *Raising Cain: Blackface Performance from Jim Crow to Hip Hop* (Cambridge, Mass.: Harvard University Press, 1998), 45.

82. Cantwell, *Bluegrass Breakdown*, 254.

83. *Variety*, Dec. 11, 1934, p. 52.

84. Douglas B. Green, "Gene Autry," in *Stars of Country Music*, ed. Bill C. Malone and Judith McCulloh (New York: Da Capo, 1991), 146.

85. Cantwell, *Bluegrass Breakdown*, 29. For a descriptive account of blackface and the *Opry*, see Charles K. Wolfe, *A Good-Natured Riot: The Birth of the Grand Ole Opry* (Nashville, Tenn.: Country Music Foundation/Vanderbilt University Press, 1999), 225–30.

86. Pamela Grundy, "'We Always Tried to Be Good People': Respectability, Crazy Water Crystals, and Hillbilly Music on the Air, 1933–35," *Journal of American History* 81:4 (Mar. 1995): 1591–1620.

87. Richard White, *"It's Your Misfortune and None of My Own": A New History of the American West* (Norman: University of Oklahoma Press, 1991), 482–83.

88. James N. Gregory, *American Exodus: The Dust Bowl Migration and Okie Culture in California* (Oxford: Oxford University Press, 1989), 102–3.

89. Grundy, "We Always Tried to Be Good People," 1611.

90. Autry's tributes are on *Memories of Jimmie Rodgers* (Bear Family Records, BCD 15938 AH, 1997).

91. Grundy, "We Always Tried to Be Good People," 1613.

92. Michele Hilmes, *Radio Voices: American Broadcasting, 1922–1952* (Minneapolis: University of Minnesota Press, 1997), 131.

93. Sons of the Pioneers and Roy Rogers, *Songs of the Prairie* (Bear Family Records, BCD 15710 EI, 1998), essay by Laurence Zwisohn.

94. Press book for *Tumbling Tumbleweeds,* private collection of Alex Gordon.

95. Spaeth, *History of Popular Music,* 493–94.

96. Sanjek and Sanjek, *American Popular Music,* 49.

CHAPTER FOUR: COWBOY REPUBLIC

1. The years 1932 through 1934 represent a low point in the production of westerns by the Hollywood studio system and its independent satellites. From a high of 199 western features produced in 1926, production dipped slightly in 1927 and 1928 with 140-plus films produced in each of those years. In 1929, for the first time since 1923, production fell below the 100 mark. In 1930 Hollywood made just 79 Westerns, while 1931 saw a slight rise to 85, which continued in 1932, reaching 108. However, 1933 and 1934 were (until 1954) the nadir of western film production, with only 65 and 76 made, respectively. See Ed Buscombe, ed., *The BFI Companion to the Western* (London: Andre Deiutsch/British Film Institute, 1988), 426.

2. Paul Seale, "'A Host of Others': Towards a Nonlinear History of Poverty Row and the Coming of Sound," *Wide Angle* 13:1 (Jan. 1991): 80.

3. Ibid., 93.

4. W. H. Brenner, "Cozy Theater, Winchester," *Motion Picture Herald,* Nov. 30, 1935, p. 83.

5. *Motion Picture Herald,* Jan. 19, 1935, p. 83.

6. Brian Taves, "The B Film: Hollywood's Other Half," in *The Grand Design: Hollywood as a Modern Business Enterprise, 1930–1939,* ed. Tino Balio (Berkeley: University of California Press, 1993), 322.

7. *Motion Picture Herald,* May 20, 1935, p. 26.

8. *Motion Picture Herald,* Sept. 28, 1935, p. 34.

9. *Motion Picture Herald,* June 1, 1935, p. 55.

10. C. L. Niles, "Niles Theater, Anamosa, Iowa," letter to editor, *Motion Picture Herald,* Nov. 30, 1935, p. 84.

11. Douglas Gomery, *The Hollywood Studio System* (London: Macmillan/British Film Institute, 1986), 183–84.

12. The shifts and changes in the record industry are analyzed in Russell Sanjek and David Sanjek, *American Popular Music Business in the 20th Century* (Oxford: Oxford University Press, 1991), 47–57.

13. Michele Hilmes, *Hollywood and Broadcasting: From Radio to Cable* (Urbana: University of Illinois Press, 1990), 60.

14. Press book for *Tumbling Tumbleweeds,* private collection of Alex Gordon; Sammie Jackson, "Jackson Theatre, Flomaton, Ala.: Small Town and Rural Patronage," *Motion Picture Herald,* Jan. 5, 1935, p. 60.

15. P. A. McConnell, "Emerson Theater, Hartford, Ark.," *Motion Picture Herald,* Apr. 13, 1935, p. 62.

16. M. S. Porter, "Orpheum Theater, Nelsonville, Ohio," *Motion Picture Herald,* Feb. 16, 1935, p. 72.

17. G. Carey, "Strand Theater, Paris, Ark.," *Motion Picture Herald,* Feb. 23, 1935, p. 72.

18. A. N. Miles, "Eminence Theater, Eminence, Ky.," *Motion Picture Herald,* Sept. 21, 1935, p. 53.

19. E. J. McClurg, "Grand Theater, Preston, Idaho," *Motion Picture Herald,* June 6, 1935, p. 55.

20. Charles T. Nelson, "Fay Theater, Jasper, La.," *Motion Picture Herald,* Sept. 7, 1935, p. 59.

21. Walter Holifield, "Elite Theater, Greenleaf, Kan.," *Motion Picture Herald,* Sept. 7, 1935, p. 59.

22. *Motion Picture Herald,* Feb. 1, 1936, p. 55.

23. *Motion Picture Herald,* June 15, 1935, p. 59.

24. Mary Hayes Davis, "Dixie Crewiston, Fla.," *Motion Picture Herald,* Apr. 27, 1935, p. 58.

25. J. W. Noah, "New Liberty and Ideal Theaters, Ft. Worth, Texas," *Motion Picture Herald,* June 15, 1935, p. 59.

26. *Motion Picture Herald,* Nov. 9, 1935, p. 2.

27. *Motion Picture Herald,* Dec. 7, 1935, p. 67.

28. *Motion Picture Herald,* Oct. 5, 1935, pp. 26–27.

29. *Motion Picture Herald,* Oct. 19, 1935, pp. 47.

30. Twenty-five of Bing Crosby's renditions of cowboy songs are collected on *I'm an Old Cowhand, 1933–1944* (Living Era, CD AJA 5160, 1996).

31. For the complete listings of western box-office attractions, see M. P. Smith and Ed Hulse, eds., *Don Miller's Hollywood Corral: A Comprehensive B-Western Roundup* (Burbank, Calif.: Riverwood Press, 1993), 505–16.

32. Karl Thiede, "The Bottom Line: Low Finance in the Reel West," in *Don Miller's Hollywood Corral: A Comprehensive B-Western Roundup,* ed. M. P. Smith and Ed Hulse (Burbank, Calif.: Riverwood Press, 1993), 407–26.

33. One of Salty Holmes's solo recordings, "I Want My Mama" (not an Oedipal ode but the sound the harmonica makes), can be heard on *Harmonica Masters* (Yazoo 2019, 1996).

34. Tex Ritter to Ed Finney, Aug. 1, 1939, Ed Finney Collection, Autry Museum of Western Heritage, Los Angeles.

35. Unidentified clipping, July 28, 1939, Finney Collection.

36. Undated clipping from *Variety,* Finney Collection.

37. Undated clipping from *Variety,* Finney Collection.

38. James F. Evans, *Prairie Farmer and WLS: The Burridge D. Butler Years* (Urbana: University of Illinois Press, 1969), 225.

39. Ritter to Finney, Aug. 21, 1939, Finney Collection.

40. Debbs Reynolds Interstate, "Suggestions to Improve Westerns," copy in Finney Collection.

41. Ibid.

42. Thiede, "Bottom Line," 413–14.

43. "Gene Rides Again," *New York Times,* Apr. 3, 1938.

44. Gomery, *Hollywood Studio System,* 186.

45. *Exhibitor,* Nov. 29, 1939, p. 34.

46. *Motion Picture Herald,* Apr. 22, 1939, p. 54.

47. *Motion Picture Herald,* Jan. 28, 1939, p. 50.

48. Ibid.

49. The records of Ritter's tour are held in the Finney Collection.

50. *New York Times,* Aug. 4, 1935.

51. Grace Dugan Letters, Gene Autry Collection, Autry Museum.

CHAPTER FIVE: COWBOY MINSTRELS

1. Harry Smith, ed., *Anthology of American Folk Music* (Smithsonian Folkways Recordings, SW CD 40090, 1997). Of the eight sides recorded by Ken Maynard, five have been issued on compact disc: "Fannie Moore" on *Times Ain't Like They Used to Be: Early American Rural Music, Vol. 1* (Yazoo, 2028, 1997); "Cowboy's Lament" on *When I Was a Cowboy: Early American Songs of the West, Vol. 1* (Yazoo, 2022, 1996); "Home on the Range" on *When I Was a Cowboy: Early American Songs of the West, Vol. 2* (Yazoo, 2023, 1996); and "Jesse James" on *My Rough and Rowdy Ways: Early American Rural Music—Badman Ballads and Hellraising Songs, Vol. 1* (Yazoo, 2039, 1998).

2. Greil Marcus, *Invisible Republic: Bob Dylan's Basement Tapes* (London: Picador, 1997), 111.

3. Press book for *Rootin' Tootin' Rhythm,* Autry Museum of Western Heritage, Los Angeles.

4. Press book for *Tumbling Tumbleweeds,* private collection of Alex Gordon.

5. Brooks McNamara, *Step Right Up,* rev. ed. (Jackson: University Press of Mississippi, 1995), 127–29. McNamara writes, "Because so many medicine show performers had experience with small-time vaudeville or burlesque, or with minstrel companies, sideshows or dime museums, a typical bill contained a curious collection of specialty numbers drawn from every kind of popular entertainment." But the traditional medicine show "almost invariably [ended with] a blackface 'nigger act.'"

6. Robert Cantwell, *Bluegrass Breakdown: The Making of the Old Southern Sound* (New York: Da Capo, 1992), 251–52.

7. Paul Kingsbury, ed., *The Encyclopedia of Country Music* (New York: Oxford University Press, 1998), 96.

8. W. T. Lhamon Jr., *Raising Cain: Blackface Performance from Jim Crow to Hip Hop* (Cambridge, Mass.: Harvard University Press, 1998), 144.

9. Tex Ritter's complete recordings (1932–47) are collected on *Blood on the Saddle* (Bear Family Records, BCD 16260 DI, 1999).

10. For more detail on Ritter's early career see Bill O'Neal, *Tex Ritter: America's Most Beloved Cowboy* (Austin, Tex.: Eakin, 1998), and Johnny Bond, *The Tex Ritter Story* (New York: Chappell Music, 1976).

11. "Got the Blues for Murder Only" is collected on Lonnie Johnson's *Steppin' on the Blues* (CBS Records, 467252 2, 1990).

12. *Song Hits,* Sept. 1939, pp. 18–19.

13. In *Prairie Moon* (Republic, 1938) and *Back in the Saddle Again* (Republic, 1941), Autry performs "In the Jailhouse Now," the only times that his movies featured a Jimmie Rodgers song.

14. For further discussion of Vertov's aesthetic of film as production, see Esther Sonnet, "The Politics of Representation: Modernism, Feminism, Postmodernism" (Ph.D. diss., University of Nottingham, U.K., 1993), 94–97.

15. "Gone Hollywood" appears in the press book for *Public Cowboy #1*, Gene Autry Collection, Autry Museum; the press book uses the term to highlight the differences between Autry and unnamed Hollywood stars.

16. Frank Norris, *Novels and Essays* (New York: Library of America, 1986), 337.

17. The Hoosier Hot Shots made an appearance in Autry's *In Old Monterey* (Republic, 1939).

18. William Howland Kenney, *Chicago Jazz: A Cultural History* (Oxford: Oxford University Press, 1993), 67–68.

19. "King of the Bungaloos" was reissued on *Classic Ragtime: Roots and Offshoots* (RCA Victor, 09026 63206-2, 1998).

20. "Minnie the Moocher at the Morgue" is collected on *Western Cowboy Ballads and Songs, 1925–1939* (Frémeaux et Associés, FA 034, 1995).

21. J. W. Williamson, *Hillbillyland: What the Movies Did to the Mountains and What the Mountains Did to the Movies* (Chapel Hill: University of North Carolina Press, 1995), 24. Williamson uses the court jester to make sense of the hillbilly clown, a figure that apparently did not appear in American popular culture until the end of the first quarter of the twentieth century. See pp. 38–39.

22. Press book for *Rootin' Tootin' Rhythm*.

23. Gene Autry with Michael Herskowitz, *Back in the Saddle Again* (New York: Doubleday, 1978), 66.

24. *Saturday Evening Post,* Sept. 6, 1941, clipping in Gene Autry Collection, Autry Museum. Lizzie Francke discusses Betty Burbridge in *Script Girls: Women Screenwriters in Hollywood* (London: British Film Institute, 1994), 74–75. In her filmography Francke identifies eighteen women who scripted westerns between 1930 and 1941. This is not an insignificant number, even if it does pale against the number of male writers within the genre. These women had an equally significant profile in the production of singing westerns.

25. Mary Barnsley, "Film Cowboy Picks Clothes to Please Fans," Associated Press, clipping in Autry Collection.

26. Clipping from *Screenland* (ca. 1940), scrapbook in Autry Collection.

27. Unidentified clipping, Autry Collection.

28. Unidentified clipping, Autry Collection.

29. Michael Denning, *The Cultural Front: The Laboring of American Culture in the Twentieth Century* (London: Verso, 1996), 30.

30. Richard Maltby, *Reforming the Movies* (New York: Oxford University Press, forthcoming).

31. Mary A. Bufwack and Robert K. Oermann, *Finding Her Voice: The Saga of Women in Country Music* (New York: Crown, 1993), 59.

32. For Hood's story see Bufwack and Oermann, *Finding Her Voice,* 47–49. Some of Hood's more interesting recordings, including "Calamity Jane," are compiled alongside Vernon Dalhart and Carson Robison tracks on *Wreck of the Old 97 and Other Early Hits* (CD OH 4167, 2000)

33. Bufwack and Oermann, *Finding Her Voice*, 85.

34. Tony Russell and Charles Wolfe, "Two Cowgirls of the Lone Prairie: The True Story of the Girls of the Golden West," *Old Time Music*, Winter 1986–87, pp. 6–13.

35. *Variety*, May 20, 1938, clipping in Ed Finney Collection, Autry Museum.

36. Press book for *In Old Monterey* (1939), Autry Collection.

37. Stuart Ewen and Elizabeth Ewen, *Channels of Desire: Mass Images and the Shaping of American Consciousness* (New York: McGraw-Hill, 1976); Charles Eckert, "The Carole Lombard in Macy's Window," in *Fabrications: Costume and the Female Body*, ed. Jane Gaines and Charlotte Herzog (London: Routledge, 1990), 100–121.

CHAPTER SIX: NEW DEAL COWBOYS

1. *New York Times*, Aug. 4, 1935.

2. Michael Denning, *Mechanic Accents: Dime Novels and Working-Class Culture in America* (London: Verso, 1987), 153.

3. Ibid., 72.

4. Ibid., 153.

5. Alan Trachtenberg, *The Incorporation of America: Culture and Society in the Gilded Age* (New York: Hill and Wang, 1982), 96.

6. Denning, *Mechanic Accents*, 77.

7. Bill Brown, *Reading the West: An Anthology of Dime Westerns* (New York: Bedford, 1997), 38.

8. Annemarie Bean, "Transgressing the Gender Divide: The Female Impersonator in Nineteenth-Century Blackface Minstrelsy," in *Inside the Minstrel Mask: Readings in Nineteenth-Century Blackface Minstrelsy*, ed. Annemarie Bean, James V. Hatch, and Brooks McNamara (Hanover, N.H.: Wesleyan University Press, 1996), 249, 245; Eric Lott, *Love and Theft: Blackface Minstrelsy and the American Working Class* (New York: Oxford University Press, 1993), 26.

9. David R. Roediger, *The Wages of Whiteness: Race and the Making of the American Working Class* (London: Verso, 1991); Michael Rogin, *Blackface, White Noise: Jewish Immigrants in the Hollywood Melting Pot* (Berkeley: University of California Press, 1996). See also Susan Gubar, *Racechanges: White Skin, Black Face in American Culture* (New York: Oxford University Press, 1997), 53–94, which discusses Hollywood's use of blackface in a manner similar to Rogin's discussion. I am somewhat at odds with these writers because I consider blackface performance in Hollywood's films a nostalgic invocation of an American vernacular (see Peter Stanfield, "'An Octoroon in the Kindling': American Vernacular and Blackface Minstrelsy in 1930s Hollywood," *Journal of American Studies* 31:3 [Dec. 1997]: 407–38). An edited version of this essay, retitled "From the Vulgar to the Refined: American Vernacular and Blackface Minstrelsy in *Showboat*," is collected in *Musicals: Hollywood and Beyond*, ed. Bill Marshall and Robynn Stilwell (Exeter, U.K.: Intellect Press, 2000), 147–56.

10. Dale Cockrell, *Demons of Disorder: Early Blackface Minstrels and Their World* (Cambridge: Cambridge University Press, 1997), 141.

11. W. T. Lhamon Jr., *Raising Cain: Blackface Performance from Jim Crow to Hip Hop* (Cambridge, Mass.: Harvard University Press, 1998), 179.

12. Ibid., 107.

13. Ibid.

14. Ibid., 139.

15. Ibid., 132.

16. *New York Times,* Aug. 4, 1935.

17. Richard White, *"It's Your Misfortune and None of My Own": A New History of the American West* (Norman: University of Oklahoma Press, 1991), 230.

18. John Opie, *The Law of the Land: Two Hundred Years of American Farmland Policy* (Lincoln: University of Nebraska Press, 1994), 152.

19. James N. Gregory, *American Exodus: The Dust Bowl Migration and Okie Culture in California* (New York: Oxford University Press, 1989), 75.

20. Ibid., 230.

21. Gene Autry with Michael Herskowitz, *Back in the Saddle Again* (New York: Doubleday, 1978), 53.

22. Denning, *Mechanic Accents,* 200.

23. Cockrell, *Demons of Disorder,* 169.

24. Ibid., 141.

25. *Hollywood Reporter,* Aug. 4, 1938, p. 3.

26. See press book for *Tumbling Tumbleweeds,* private collection of Alex Gordon.

27. Denning discusses the cultural responses to these strikes in *The Cultural Front: The Laboring of American Culture in the Twentieth Century* (London: Verso, 1996), 259–82.

28. Charles Eckert, "The Anatomy of a Proletarian Film: Warner's *Marked Woman,"* in *Movies and Methods,* vol. 2, ed. Bill Nichols (Berkeley: University of California Press, 1985), 407–25.

29. Packy Smith and Ed Hulse, eds., *Don Miller's Hollywood Corral: A Comprehensive B-Western Roundup* (Burbank, Calif.: Riverwood Press, 1993), 177.

30. For a discussion of detective agencies in turn-of-the-century popular fiction, see Marcus Klein, *Easterns, Westerns, and Private Eyes: American Matters, 1870–1900* (Madison: University of Wisconsin Press, 1994), 133–54.

CONCLUSION

1. *New York Times,* Aug. 6, 1939.

2. Paul Holt, *Daily Express* (London), reproduced in *Republic Reporter,* Oct. 1, 1939, n.p., private collection of Alex Gordon. Max Miller was a popular English comedian.

3. Ibid.

4. W. C. Handy describes this concert in his 1941 autobiography, *Father of the Blues* (rpt., New York: Da Capo, 1991), 299–304.

INDEX

PETER STANFIELD is a lecturer on the media arts faculty at Southampton Institute (U.K.) and the author of *Hollywood, Westerns, and the 1930s: The Lost Trail* (2001). He is working on another book, tentatively titled *A Selection from the Gutter,* which considers how classical Hollywood used popular songs—such as "Frankie and Johnny," "St. Louis Blues," "Blues in the Night," "The Man I Love," and "Body and Soul"—as part of its production of an American vernacular.

The University of Illinois Press
is a founding member of the
Association of American University Presses.

———————————————————

Composed in 10.5/13 New Baskerville
with Minion, Giddyup Thangs display
by Jim Proefrock
at the University of Illinois Press
Designed by Paula Newcomb
Manufactured by Thomson-Shore, Inc.

University of Illinois Press
1325 South Oak Street
Champaign, IL 61820-6903
www.press.uillinois.edu